Preparation for

TOTAL CONSECRATION

TO JESUS CHRIST THROUGH MARY

Nihil Obstat
Text taken from approved and traditional sources.
REV. MSGR. ROBERT O. MORRISSEY, J.C.D.,
Censor Liborum
26 February 2012

Imprimatur
+MOST REVEREND WILLIAM MURPHY,
Bishop of Rockville Centre
28 February 2012

Imprimi Potest
MATTHEW CONSIDINE, S.M.M.,
Provincial Superior

Preparation for

TOTAL CONSECRATION

TO JESUS CHRIST THROUGH MARY

────────

ACCORDING TO ST. LOUIS DE MONTFORT

Prepared by

FR. HUGH GILLESPIE, S.M.M.

MONTFORT PUBLICATIONS

Ad Jesum per Mariam

New York

Paperback
6th Printing: 2013

Montfort Publications
26 South Saxon Avenue, Bay Shore, NY 11706
www.montfortpublications.com

Montfort Publications is a ministry of the Missionaries of the Company of Mary (Montfort Missionaries). The Montfort Publications name and logo are trademarks of the Montfort Missionaries.

ISBN-10: 0-910984-07-7
ISBN-13: 978-0-910984-07-2

Printed in the United States of America

Book & Cover design by David Lopez
Cover photo © 2011 Hugh Gillespie, S.M.M.

"It is through the Most Holy Virgin Mary
that Jesus Christ has come to the world,
and it is also through her
that he must reign in the world."

– *St. Louis de Montfort*

*Statue of Mary, Queen of All Hearts, from the church of
Maria Regina dei Cuori, Rome, Italy.*

This work is dedicated to

Fr. Roger Charest, S.M.M. and Fr. J. Patrick Gaffney, S.M.M.
who labored so long and so well through the years
on behalf of Our Lady.

OUR LADY, QUEEN OF ALL HEARTS, PRAY FOR THEM!

ACKNOWLEDGMENTS

With grateful acknowledgment to the staff of Montfort Publications, especially David Lopez for his fine work on the layout and overall graphic design of the book and Edith Matlock for her diligence in moving the book to publication; and to our proof readers, Barbara Sanford, Kathryn Rodgers, and David and Valerie Calvillo, whose attention to detail and insightful feedback have greatly enhanced the final text: May Our Lady, the Queen of All Hearts, bless each of you and your families with that sure and certain peace and consolation that flow in such generous abundance from the Heart of her Son.

INDEX OF PRAYERS

Additional Prayers are listed on the Contents page.

ABBREVIATIONS
Used in referring to the works of St. Louis de Montfort.

FC   Letter to the Friends of the Cross
L   Letters
LEW   The Love of Eternal Wisdom
MR   Methods for Saying the Rosary
SM   The Secret of Mary
SR   The Secret of the Rosary
TD   True Devotion to the Blessed Virgin Mary

CONTENTS

Photo of the Immaculate Heart of Mary stained glass window from
St. Katharine Drexel Parish (formerly St. Michael's Parish), Lansford, PA.

FOREWORD

"I feel a tremendous urge to make our Lord and his holy Mother loved, to go in a humble and simple way to teach catechism to the poor in country places and to arouse in sinners a devotion to our Blessed Lady... I know very well, my dear Father, that I am not worthy to do such honorable work, but when I see the needs of the Church I cannot help pleading continually for a small and poor band of good priests to do this work under the banner and protection of the Blessed Virgin."

– St. Louis de Montfort

St. Louis Marie Grignion de Montfort, the great French missionary and preacher, burned with a deep and genuine vocational zeal for the renewal of the Church through the vigorous proclamation of the Gospel. For him the secret of effective proclamation of the Gospel and the secret of authentic living of the Gospel are one and the same, and the name of this secret is Mary. This is because Christian life fully and truly lived is nothing less than a radically powerful and intimate participation in the life of Jesus Christ himself. Father de Montfort insisted that full participation in the life of Jesus requires a relationship with Mary. Therefore, those who truly sought to grow into the full maturity of life in Jesus Christ could find no more sure or certain or reliable means of doing so than by surrendering themselves fully into the care of the great Mother of God in the same way that the Lord himself has done *who did not consider equality with God something to be grasped, but made himself nothing, taking the very nature of a servant, being made in human likeness* (Phil 2: 6-7) – for us and for our salvation.

St. Louis de Montfort recognized this simple and compelling truth as being the very foundation upon which a renewed Church must be established. So convinced was he of this that, nearly three centuries before the Second Vatican Council's sustained development of the universal call to holiness of all the faithful, he could boldly assert to those who turned to him for guidance "Chosen soul....it is certain that growth in the holiness of God is your vocation." Fr. de Montfort devoted all of the energy of his vocational life to living and proclaiming a true devotion to Our Lady as the most powerful and direct means of becoming fully mature in the Spirit of Jesus Christ. This True Devotion to the Blessed Virgin that St. Louis de Montfort proposes is a path of radical self-surrender to the Almighty that he calls Total Consecration.

The spiritual legacy contained within the life and writings of St. Louis de Montfort is one of the truly great treasures of the Church. The task of bringing the full wealth of that treasure to the faithful is the heart of the mission of the Company of Mary, the community of those priests and brothers who have been consecrated to follow in his footsteps. This book has been prepared by the Company of Mary in the United States to serve as a point of contact and education for those who feel called to risk a fuller living out of their baptismal immersion in the life of Jesus Christ by means of making a total consecration of themselves to this same Jesus Christ, our Lord and our Savior, through the hands of the Blessed Virgin Mary, the Queen of All Hearts.

Ad Jesum per Mariam

Fr. Hugh Gillespie, S.M.M.
Feast of the Queenship of Mary
22 August 2011

AN INTRODUCTION TO
TOTAL CONSECRATION

TOTUS TUUS EGO SUM.

I am all yours, O my Jesus,
and all that I have is yours
through Mary,
your most holy Mother.

— *St. Louis de Montfort*

TOTAL CONSECRATION

The Basis for Total Consecration

St. Louis de Montfort recognized that at its very foundation Christian life is nothing less than a participation in the life of Jesus Christ. Through baptism we belong completely to Christ; and holiness, therefore, is the common vocation of all Christians.

The spirituality of total consecration that St. Louis de Montfort proposes bases itself in this reality which is the central mystery of Christianity: *by means of his Incarnation and Cross, Jesus Christ has saved us and has made us true children of God the Father, filled with his Holy Spirit.* This is to say, Jesus, the Son of God the Father, has shared in our human condition in every way so that we may be given a sharing in his Divine life. This sharing of Jesus is not a partial sharing, but a complete sharing. He has given himself to us even to the point of sharing our dying so that we may share in everything with him.

This sharing includes his relationship with Mary because he who is truly the Son of the Almighty Father is also the son of Mary. Furthermore, because Jesus has given himself completely to us through Mary, those who wish to give themselves completely to Christ must do the same. Through Mary salvation came into our world and through Mary we can experience the fullness of this same salvation which is nothing less than a total sharing, a profound participation, in the life of Jesus Christ. In the words of Father de Montfort, no one can truly be a child of God the Father without also being a child of Mary.

An Important Question
Does giving so much importance to Mary distract us from Jesus?

ST. LOUIS DE MONTFORT WRITES, "IF WE SEEK TO ESTABLISH A true and solid devotion to the most holy Virgin, it is only in order to more perfectly establish devotion to Jesus Christ and to offer a secure and easy means of coming to him. This devotion is necessary for us to perfectly reach Jesus Christ, to love him with tenderness and to serve him with fidelity." This is because "The strongest tendency of Mary is to unite us to Jesus Christ, her Son, and the greatest desire of her Son is that we come to him by means of his most holy Mother." Recognizing this, Fr. de Montfort insisted that "The one who desires to possess fruit that is ripe and beautifully formed must have access to the tree that produces it. Whoever desires the fruit of life – Jesus Christ – must possess the tree of life which is Mary. Whoever desires that the Holy Spirit move powerfully within him must have his inseparable spouse, Mary most holy." And, in even stronger terms, "I personally believe that no one can arrive at a truly intimate union with our Lord and a perfect fidelity to the Holy Spirit without a very profound union with the most holy Virgin and a true dependence upon her support."

The great servant of God, Blessed John Paul II, found in St. Louis de Montfort's masterpiece, *True Devotion to the Blessed Virgin Mary*, the answer to this very question. He writes: "Whereas previously I held back for fear that devotion to Mary would obscure Christ rather than give him precedence, I understood with the light of (St. Louis de Montfort's) book that in truth it was entirely different..... We might even say that Christ himself appoints his Mother to those who strive to know and to love him, as he did on Calvary with his disciple John." Pope John Paul II's esteem for the fruits of the spirituality of consecration that he learned from St. Louis de Montfort was so great that he made Fr. de Montfort's *Totus Tuus* (I am all yours) his papal motto.

Preparing to make the Total Consecration

IF FR. DE MONTFORT'S *ACT OF TOTAL CONSECRATION* WERE SIMPLY A prayer to be said as the result of one's devotional fervor, there would be no real need to undertake a serious preparation process, let alone one that lasts for more than a month. For St. Louis de Montfort, however, consecration is not the gesture of a moment, but a radical surrender of oneself into the life of Jesus Christ. It is Christian Spirituality in the fullest sense of the word. The *Act of Total Consecration*, therefore, as that moment in which one formally makes this act of surrender, is a first step, a beginning, that one must then deepen and renew and express in the faithful living of one's consecration on a daily basis. A step like this is a step that one must prepare himself to take.

At base, the process of preparation consists of two movements – emptying oneself of the spirit of the world and filling oneself with the spirit of Jesus Christ. These are the two basic movements of Montfort spirituality.

In order to make the first movement, one sets aside at least twelve days to learn to recognize the spirit of the world and its effect upon our lives. One struggles against this spirit and its false wisdom by means of prayer and mortification in order to perceive more clearly the light of the Gospel. After renouncing the spirit of the world one cannot remain empty, and, therefore, one must become filled with the Spirit of Jesus Christ.

This second movement unfolds by means of three related steps:

• One week dedicated to coming to a more profound knowledge of ourselves during which we wish to become truly aware of our tendencies to sin and to acquire a spirit of genuine humility.

• One week dedicated to coming to a more profound knowledge of the Virgin Mary during which we wish to more fully open our lives to her presence.

• One week dedicated to coming to a more profound knowledge of Jesus Christ in which we seek to permit the light of our knowledge of ourselves and our knowledge of Mary to illuminate our relationship to Jesus so that we may participate more fully in his life and mission.

Knowledge in each of these cases does not refer simply to intellectual and catechetical knowledge— these are both necessary and desirable but, by themselves fall short of what St. Louis de Montfort is asking of us. Rather, the knowledge of which Fr. de Montfort speaks is personal knowledge. In other words, for example, we are asked to spend time not simply increasing our knowledge about Mary, but to come to know her personally.

Each of these periods will be marked by a set of daily reflections, prayers, and resolutions that are designed to allow one to learn and begin to live the fundamental elements of St. Louis de Montfort's spirituality of total consecration prior to making the *Act of Total Consecration*. As there is a distinct fruit that each of these periods produces within us, each of them will begin and end with a formal act of prayer in addition to the exercises that are assigned to the individual days. The heart of this process is found in the prayerful meditation upon each day's readings – which are taken from the scriptures and the writings of St. Louis de Montfort – and in concrete responses one makes as a result of this meditation.

The process of preparation lasts for thirty-three days. This is a symbolic number. Tradition holds that the Lord Jesus lived among us for thirty-three years before his saving Death and Resurrection, and so a time of thirty-three days represents the fullness of his Life in which we long to fully share. At the conclusion of these thirty-three days, usually on the thirty-fourth day, one makes the personal *Act of Total Consecration.* To the extent that it is possible, this process should be brought to a grace-filled conclusion by uniting it to the celebration of the Eucharist. One should celebrate the Sacrament of Reconciliation prior to making the *Act of Total Consecration.* One can go through this process privately and individually and one can also unite with a group.

Choosing a Feast Day

It is wise to take some time to consider when one would like to make the *Act of Total Consecration,* as so significant a step in one's spiritual life should be made carefully. On a practical level, should the demands of life be such that one cannot reliably set aside the time necessary to be faithful to the process of preparation, it is better to choose a later date and then make whatever concrete changes one must to assure that it is possible to then give the preparation process the attention it deserves. Furthermore, one must be attentive to the fact that certain times of the year may not be conducive to the taking of time for a focused series of spiritual exercises beyond one's normal daily prayers. For example, periods of heavy travel for work, an annual family vacation, end of semester exams, and other such occasions demand a considerable focus of time and energy and one must be attentive to this in choosing a time that is truly appropriate for undertaking additional spiritual exercises.

In choosing a time that is conducive to undertaking the process of preparation, one should also take some care in selecting a feast day from the Church's liturgical calendar upon which to make the *Act of Total Consecration* itself. While one may, in fact, freely make his *Act of Total Consecration* on any day of the year, it is most fitting that the giving of oneself, in the spirit of Jesus, into the hands of Our Lady be done on one of her feast days. A list of suggested feast days is included at the end of this book. The date of one's *Act of Total Consecration* will become that person's feast day as well, a day to be celebrated and upon which one will renew his *Act of Total Consecration* each year. In the words of Fr. de Montfort himself, that one feast day which captures more fully than any other the very essence of this devotion of consecration is the feast of the Incarnation (the Annunciation) which is celebrated on the 25th day of March. Because of its importance to St. Louis de Montfort, many will therefore seek to make the *Act of Total Consecration* on this date.

Once the feast day is chosen, what is frequently done is that one then counts back the thirty-three days before it to determine the starting date for the preparation process (the feast day being day thirty-four). However, it is often advisable to leave a few days between the last day of the preparation process and the date of consecration to allow one the opportunity to make a good confession or to prayerfully reflect upon the fruits of the preparation process. While it is not necessary for the consecration date to follow immediately upon the conclusion of the preparation process, one should not allow more than a week to pass between the preparation process and the date of one's *Act of Total Consecration*.

The making of the *Act of Total Consecration* is a significant moment in one's spiritual life and the occasion should be treated as such. During the preparation process one should begin planning how the day itself will be kept. Is it possible, for example, to take the day off from work? Will one need to free up time to attend Mass? After making the *Act of Total Consecration*, how will one celebrate? Is there a danger of the day of Consecration itself simply being too busy to allow for a period of truly reflective prayer? It is very important that while one is faithfully and attentively working through the daily exercises of this preparation process that he does not lose sight of the need to prepare the day of his Consecration as well.

Holy Slavery

ACCORDING TO ST. LOUIS DE MONTFORT, TOTAL CONSECRATION must be understood in terms of a total surrender of oneself to Our Lady so that one might belong totally and without reservation to the Lord Jesus Christ. Because of this insistence on a radically complete, a total, belonging to Our Lord and Our Lady, he frequently uses the term "Holy Slavery" as another name for his spirituality of consecration. Slavery is a problematic and off-putting term for many and Fr. de Montfort's use of it can be easily misunderstood. It is also a very important part of the great saint's spiritual vocabulary. It is likewise a very important part of the biblical witness both to the person of Jesus who, for our salvation, *emptied himself, taking the form of a slave* (Phil 2:7) and to the life of faithful discipleship – St. Paul, for example, refers to himself on numerous occasions as a *slave of Christ Jesus*. It is necessary, therefore, that the notion of Holy Slavery be properly understood.

Slavery understood in worldly, social and political terms is a degrading and dehumanizing reality that treats human beings as little more than objects to be bought, sold and used. It is coercive, oppressive and implemented and maintained by violent means. Despite the abolition of violent and sinful official structures of slavery in most of the world, there remains much, however, that can enslave the human person in ways that, while less outwardly obvious, are very real and often very violent in their hold upon us. Addiction is one such thing. So too are the relentless insecurities and fearful preoccupations which so readily rob so many of the simple and fundamental freedom to choose and to act as they know they should. Lingering resentments and old wounds wind themselves around the human heart like many chains, diminishing its ability to feel and to love. And then there is our persistent sinfulness - the vices that dominate us and the temptations that all too easily and too frequently overwhelm and overcome us all the while whispering the seductive lie that we are truly free. This slavery, this belonging to that which overpowers and diminishes our true dignity, is not holy, but it is an all too real aspect of our lives.

Unfortunately, it is often the case that in seeking to be freed from the many powers that can so readily dominate us that we follow a false, and ultimately destructive, path. There are many ways that at first glance offer us freedom only to produce little more than another form, often worse, of oppressive servitude. This too is one of the painful realities of human experience – all too often in seeking freedom one gives himself over into the hands of a false savior and ends up belonging to another demeaning master. Fr. de Montfort knew well how deeply the human heart longs for true and lasting freedom, the freedom of the children of God. He also knew that this freedom can only be found in Jesus Christ. One must, according to St. Louis de Montfort, belong to Jesus Christ or one must find himself enslaved to the powers of this world. The more fully one belongs to Jesus Christ, the more fully one surrenders himself into the possession of Jesus Christ, the more fully that person will be truly free with the freedom of the children of God.

Belonging to Jesus Christ, a total belonging, a total surrender of one's very self to Jesus Christ is what Fr. de Montfort means when he uses the expression Holy Slavery. A total surrender such as this can only be made in love as it is nothing other than a complete giving of oneself over to another. This radical act of giving is not coerced; it is done in freedom. And it produces a belonging to and a dependence upon Our Lord and Our Lady that is so total that

St. Louis de Montfort can find no more fitting word to describe it than "slavery." It is also an unspeakably intimate participation in the life of Jesus himself who completely surrenders himself, for us and our salvation, into the hands of the Blessed Virgin and to the will of his Father. Fr. de Montfort emphasizes this in the very words of the Act of Total Consecration:

> Receive, O benign Virgin,
> this little offering of my slavery,
> in honor of, and in union with, the submission
> that eternal Wisdom deigned to have to your maternity.....

It is only in belonging to Jesus Christ that one is truly free for it brings us the true freedom of the children of God. This is the one slavery that can justly and truly be named Holy.

Prayers to be said each day

St. Louis de Montfort insists that those who wish to consecrate themselves to Jesus Christ by means of Mary must submit themselves to the direction of the Holy Spirit. Therefore, each day of the process of preparation will begin with the *Invocation of the Holy Spirit*. Furthermore, because we seek to consecrate ourselves to Jesus Christ who comes to us always and everywhere as the fruit of Mary, each day we will also recite the prayer *Jesus living in Mary*. It is very important to learn these prayers and to make them part of our spiritual life because they touch directly upon very fundamental aspects of Montfort's spirituality of consecration.

INVOCATION OF THE HOLY SPIRIT

V   Come Holy Spirit, fill the hearts of your faithful
R   And enkindle in them the fire of your love.

V   Lord, send forth your Spirit.
R   And you will renew the face of the earth.

O God,
who instructs the hearts of your faithful
with the light of your Holy Spirit,
make us responsive to his inspirations
so that we may be truly wise and
ever rejoice in his consolations.
Through Christ our Lord.
Amen.

Jesus Living in Mary

O Jesus living in Mary,
come and live in your servant
in the Spirit of your holiness,
in the fullness of your gifts,
in the perfection of your ways,
in the truth of your virtues,
in the communion of your mysteries.
Subdue within me the power of flesh and demon
by your Holy Spirit, for the glory of God the Father.
Amen.

In addition to these two prayers, each stage of the process will have a specific prayer to say as a night prayer at the closing of the day. The night prayer is meant to be brief, but it is an important element of this process in that it calls us to be attentive to the ways we engage and appropriate the particular spiritual movements of the exercises in our daily activity.

The text of those prayers will be found with the material prepared for those particular stages.

Statue of St. Louis de Montfort from
St. Mary Gate of Heaven Parish, Ozone Park, NY.

RENUNCIATION OF
THE SPIRIT OF THE WORLD

———————

*The spirit of the world is opposed
to the spirit of Jesus Christ.*

A SPIRIT OPPOSED TO THE GOSPEL

St. Louis de Montfort writes, "Those who desire to take up this devotion should spend at least twelve days emptying themselves of the spirit of the world, which is opposed to the spirit of Jesus." Twelve days will prove to be too little time, barring a tremendous gift of grace, for any of us to fully cast off the spirit of the world, but it is a sufficient amount of time to make a good beginning of doing so. Recognizing that those who would fully surrender themselves to the Lord Jesus will spend much of their lives deepening their renunciation of the false values of the world so that they may be more fully filled with the spirit of the Gospel, these first twelve days are a crucial element of the preparation process as it is here that we become firm in our commitment to lay aside what is false and to live according to the light of Truth. It is likewise here that we come to terms with just how much of our lives has been colored, controlled and determined by the self-seeking and self-centered spirit of the world and what concrete choices we must make to truly embrace the self-giving and self-sacrificing spirit of Jesus Christ.

The spirit of the world is self-centered. The spirit of the world is self-seeking. The spirit of the world is self-serving. The spirit of the world is self-aggrandizing. The spirit of the world is selfish, self-absorbed and self-interested. St. Louis de Montfort teaches that self-denial is a powerful and necessary means of combating the self-absorption and self-interest of the worldly spirit. To this end, in addition to consciously setting aside the time required to faithfully attend to the daily spiritual exercises required of the preparation process, those preparing to make the *Act of Total Consecration* will be asked during these twelve days (on day three) to make a concrete act of sacrifice for the duration of their time of preparation. This is similar to the penitential custom of "giving something up for Lent" that is a familiar and valuable element of the Catholic tradition. The sacrifice that is made does not have to be great, but it does have to be a genuine act of self-denial that will be felt. In much the same way that our penitential self-denial during Lent sharpens our spiritual focus during that holy season and helps to prepare us to celebrate the Paschal Mystery of the Lord's victory over sin and death, acts of self-denial begin to turn us away from worldly self-assertion and prepare us to make a genuine surrender of ourselves to Jesus through Mary.

Another very important element of these first twelve days, which we will face on day two, is the need to make a firm commitment to the daily aspect of the preparation process. The demands and distractions of daily life are many, and they can easily crowd out the time we intend to set aside for spiritual growth if we are not careful. The temptation to put off doing the readings and exercises until later, until tomorrow, until one has free time which never comes, will be considerable. Likewise the temptation to skip a day or to combine two or more days of exercises together, or to simply fit the exercises in where one can will be difficult to resist if one is not prepared to do so. A fixed amount of time at a regular hour is important. If we are unable to consecrate a small amount of our time to the Lord with any regularity, we will not be ready to truly make a gift of ourselves to him at the end of these thirty-three days. It is important that we be reasonable in doing this, however. It is better to set aside a smaller amount of time, for example twenty minutes, that one can actually keep on a daily basis than to attempt to set aside an hour which he will not be able to keep faithfully.

For Night Prayer over these twelve days one is asked to simply pause a few moments in prayerful reflection that recalls the theme of the day and the fruits of one's meditation upon it. One then places himself and his struggle against the spirit of the world under the protective care of Our Lady by praying the *Sub Tuum* one of the most ancient prayers imploring her maternal intercession:

SUB TUUM

We fly to your patronage,
O holy Mother of God.
Despise not our petitions in our necessities,
but deliver us always from all dangers,
O glorious and blessed Virgin.
Amen.

At the very beginning of the preparation process, as one prepares to struggle against the spirit of the world which is opposed to the spirit of Jesus Christ, and before beginning the first day's spiritual exercises, it is important to invoke the grace of God upon this effort. Those who seek to empty themselves of the spirit of the world so that they may be filled by the spirit of Jesus Christ call upon his aid— *Our help is in the name of the Lord*—by praying *the Litany of the Holy Name of Jesus.* While one is certainly free to make the Litany part of his daily prayer over these twelve days, it is only necessary to pray it at the very beginning.

Upon completing the exercises for the twelfth day, one places the fruits of this time in the hands of the Blessed Virgin by praying the *Ave Maris Stella,* a prayer that Fr. de Montfort esteemed greatly.

LITANY OF THE HOLY NAME

To make a fitting beginning to the process of preparation, it is best to pray this litany before, or while holding, a crucifix.

Lord, have mercy	Lord, have mercy
Christ, have mercy	Christ, have mercy
Lord, have mercy	Lord, have mercy
God our Father in heaven	have mercy on us
God the Son, Redeemer of the world	have mercy on us
God the Holy Spirit	have mercy on us
Holy Trinity, one God	have mercy on us
Jesus, Son of the living God	have mercy on us
Jesus, splendor of the Father	have mercy on us
Jesus, brightness of everlasting light	have mercy on us
Jesus, king of glory	have mercy on us
Jesus, dawn of justice	have mercy on us
Jesus, Son of the Virgin Mary	have mercy on us
Jesus, worthy of our love	have mercy on us
Jesus, worthy of our wonder	have mercy on us
Jesus, mighty God	have mercy on us
Jesus, father of the world to come	have mercy on us
Jesus, prince of peace	have mercy on us
Jesus, all-powerful	have mercy on us
Jesus, pattern of patience	have mercy on us
Jesus, model of obedience	have mercy on us
Jesus, gentle and humble of heart	have mercy on us
Jesus, lover of chastity	have mercy on us
Jesus, lover of us all	have mercy on us
Jesus, God of peace	have mercy on us

Jesus, author of life	have mercy on us
Jesus, model of goodness	have mercy on us
Jesus, seeker of souls	have mercy on us
Jesus, our God	have mercy on us
Jesus, our refuge	have mercy on us
Jesus, father of the poor	have mercy on us
Jesus, treasure of the faithful	have mercy on us
Jesus, Good Shepherd	have mercy on us
Jesus, the true light	have mercy on us
Jesus, eternal wisdom	have mercy on us
Jesus, infinite goodness	have mercy on us
Jesus, our way and our life	have mercy on us
Jesus, joy of angels	have mercy on us
Jesus, king of patriarchs	have mercy on us
Jesus, teacher of apostles	have mercy on us
Jesus, master of evangelists	have mercy on us
Jesus, courage of martyrs	have mercy on us
Jesus, light of confessors	have mercy on us
Jesus, purity of virgins	have mercy on us
Jesus, crown of all saints	have mercy on us
Lord, be merciful	Jesus, save your people
From all evil	Jesus, save your people
From every sin	Jesus, save your people
From the snares of the devil	Jesus, save your people
From your anger	Jesus, save your people
From the spirit of infidelity	Jesus, save your people
From everlasting death	Jesus, save your people
From neglect of your Holy Spirit	Jesus, save your people

By the mystery of your incarnation	Jesus, save your people
By your birth	Jesus, save your people
By your childhood	Jesus, save your people
By your hidden life	Jesus, save your people
By your public ministry	Jesus, save your people
By your agony and crucifixion	Jesus, save your people
By your abandonment	Jesus, save your people
By your grief and sorrow	Jesus, save your people
By your death and burial	Jesus, save your people
By your rising to new life	Jesus, save your people
By your return in glory to the Father	Jesus, save your people
By your gift of the Holy Eucharist	Jesus, save your people
By your joy and glory	Jesus, save your people

Christ, hear us   Christ, hear us
Lord Jesus, hear our prayer Lord Jesus, hear our prayer

Lamb of God,
 you take away the sins of the world have mercy on us
Lamb of God,
 you take away the sins of the world have mercy on us
Lamb of God,
 you take away the sins of the world have mercy on us

 Lord,
 may we who honor the holy name of Jesus
 enjoy his friendship in this life
 and be filled with eternal joy in the kingdom
 where he lives and reigns for ever and ever.
 Amen.

DAY ONE
Do not Conform to the Spirit of this Age

Prayer: INVOCATION OF THE HOLY SPIRIT (PG. 12)

Scripture   *Romans 12: 1-2*

I appeal to you, brothers and sisters, by the mercies of God, to present your bodies as a living sacrifice, holy and acceptable to God, which is your spiritual worship. Do not be conformed to the spirit of this world, but be transformed by the renewing of your mind, that you may prove what is the will of God, what is good and acceptable and perfect.

St. Louis de Montfort   *SM: #3*

Chosen soul, living image of God and redeemed by the precious blood of Jesus Christ, God wants you to be holy like him in this life, and glorious like him in the next. It is certain that growth in holiness is your vocation. All your thoughts, words, and actions, everything you suffer or undertake must lead you to that end. Otherwise, you are resisting God in not doing the work for which he created you and for which even now he is keeping you in being. What a marvelous transformation is possible! Dust into light, uncleanness into purity, sinfulness into holiness, creature into Creator, man into God! A marvelous work, I repeat, so difficult in itself, even impossible for a mere creature to bring about, for only God can accomplish it by giving his grace abundantly and in an extraordinary manner. The very creation of the universe is not as great an achievement as this.

---

[1] The guides will show the day you are on in the overall 33 day process.

Question

How would you describe this vocation to holiness that St. Louis de Montfort speaks about?

Prayer: JESUS LIVING IN MARY (PG. 13)

Night Prayer: SUB TUUM (PG. 18)

DAY TWO
We must Count the Cost

Prayer: INVOCATION OF THE HOLY SPIRIT (PG. 12)

Scripture   *Luke 14: 28-30*

For which of you, desiring to build a tower, does not first sit down and count the cost, whether he has enough to complete it? Otherwise, when he has laid a foundation, and is not able to finish, all who see it begin to mock him, saying, 'This man began to build and was not able to finish.'

St. Louis de Montfort   *SM: #4*

Chosen soul, how will you bring this about? What steps will you take to reach the high level to which God is calling you? The means of holiness and salvation are known to everybody, since they are found in the gospel; the masters of the spiritual life have explained them; the saints have practiced them and shown how essential they are for those who wish to be saved and attain perfection. These means are: sincere humility, unceasing prayer, complete self-denial, abandonment to divine Providence, and obedience to the will of God.

Question

In order to continue with the process of preparation it is necessary to determine how much time each day you will dedicate to the personal prayer and meditation that is required. This must be a firm commitment that you intend to keep for the entire preparation period. It is not possible to genuinely complete the process of preparation without taking this step.

Prayer: Jesus Living in Mary (pg. 13)

Night Prayer: Sub Tuum (pg. 18)

DAY THREE
One must Sacrifice for the Kingdom

Prayer: INVOCATION OF THE HOLY SPIRIT (PG. 12)

Scripture   *Mark 10: 24-30*

But Jesus said to them again, "Children, how hard it is for those who trust in riches to enter the kingdom of God! It is easier for a camel to go through the eye of a needle than for a rich man to enter the kingdom of God." And they were exceedingly astonished and said to him, "Then who can be saved?" Jesus looked at them and said, "With men it is impossible, but not with God; for all things are possible with God." Peter began to say to him, "Behold, we have left everything and followed you." Jesus said, "Truly I say to you, there is no one who has left house or brothers or sisters or mother or father or children or lands, for my sake and for the gospel, who will not receive a hundredfold now in this time, houses and brothers and sisters and mothers and children and lands, with persecutions, and in the age to come eternal life.

St. Louis de Montfort   *LEW: #194*

The Holy Spirit tells us that Wisdom is not found in the hearts of those who live in comfort, gratifying their passions and bodily desires, because "they who are of the flesh cannot please God," and "the wisdom of the flesh is an enemy to God". "My spirit will not remain in man, because he is flesh."

All those who belong to Christ, incarnate Wisdom, have crucified their flesh with its passions and desires. They always bear about in their bodies the dying of Jesus. They continually do violence to themselves, carry their cross daily. They are dead and indeed buried with Christ.

These words of the Holy Spirit show us more clearly than the light of day that, if we are to possess incarnate Wisdom, Jesus Christ, we must practice self-denial and renounce the world and self.

Resolution

Daily sacrifice is also a necessary component of the process of preparation – as necessary and important as consistent daily prayer and reflection. Do not continue until you have decided upon an act of sacrifice that you can make over the remainder of the period of preparation. This must be a firm decision to which you intend to be faithful.

Prayer: JESUS LIVING IN MARY (PG. 13)

Night Prayer: SUB TUUM (PG. 18)

DAY FOUR
The Worldly make Excuses

Prayer: INVOCATION OF THE HOLY SPIRIT (PG. 12)

Scripture   *Luke 14: 16-24*

But he said to him, "A man once gave a great banquet, and invited many; and at the time for the banquet he sent his servant to say to those who had been invited, 'Come; for all is now ready.' But they all alike began to make excuses. The first said to him, 'I have bought a field, and I must go out and see it; please, have me excused.' And another said, 'I have bought five yoke of oxen, and I go to examine them; please, have me excused.' And another said, 'I have married a wife, and therefore I cannot come.' So the servant came and reported this to his master. Then the householder in anger said to his servant, 'Go out quickly to the streets and lanes of the city and bring in the poor and maimed and blind and lame.' And the servant said, 'Sir, what you commanded has been done, and there is still room.' And the master said to the servant, 'Go out to the highways and hedges, and compel people to come in, that my house may be filled. For I tell you, none of those men who were invited will taste my banquet.'

St. Louis de Montfort   *LEW: #76*

In the opinion of the world, a wise man is one with a keen eye to business; who knows how to turn everything to his personal profit without appearing to do so. He excels in the art of duplicity and well-concealed fraud without arousing suspicion. He thinks one thing and says another. Nothing concerning the graces and manners of the world is unknown to him. He accommodates himself to everyone to suit his end, completely ignoring the honor and interests of God. He manages to make a secret but fatal reconciliation of truth and false-hood, of the gospel and the world, of Christ and Belial. He wishes to be considered an honest man but not a devout man, and most readily scorns, distorts and condemns devotions he does not person-ally approve of. In short, a man is worldly-wise who, following solely the lead of his senses and human reasoning, poses as a good Christian and a man of integrity, but makes little effort to please God or atone by penance for the sins he has committed against him.

Question

The temptation to make excuses for not responding to the will and the call of God is very common and very subtle. What are the excuses that you make most frequently?

Prayer: JESUS LIVING IN MARY (PG. 13)

Night Prayer: SUB TUUM (PG. 18)

DAY FIVE
Enter through the Narrow Gate

Prayer: INVOCATION OF THE HOLY SPIRIT (PG. 12)

Scripture   *Matthew 7:13-14*

Enter by the narrow gate; for the gate is wide and the way is easy that leads to destruction, and those who enter it are many. For the gate is narrow and the way is hard, that leads to life, and those who find it are few.

St. Louis de Montfort   *FC #5*

Are you walking along the true way of life, which is the narrow and stony way of Calvary? Or are you, without perhaps realizing it, on the wide road of the world which leads to perdition? Are you aware that there is a highway which is to all appearances a straight and safe road, but which really leads to eternal death?

Question

Take some time with these questions of St. Louis de Montfort. Are you truly faithful to the Gospel even when doing what is right is unpopular, or do you tend to take the easier path of compromising its fullness to remain at peace with the world?

Prayer: JESUS LIVING IN MARY (PG. 13)

Night Prayer: SUB TUUM (PG. 18)

Day Six
The Worldly are Hypocritical

Prayer: INVOCATION OF THE HOLY SPIRIT (PG. 12)

Scripture *Matthew 23: 25-28*

Woe to you, scribes and Pharisees, hypocrites! for you cleanse the outside of the cup and of the plate, but inside they are full of extortion and rapacity. You blind Pharisee! first cleanse the inside of the cup and of the plate, that the outside also may be clean. Woe to you, scribes and Pharisees, hypocrites! for you are like whitewashed tombs, which outwardly appear beautiful, but within they are full of dead men's bones and all uncleanness. So also you outwardly appear righteous to men, but within you are full of hypocrisy and iniquity.

St. Louis de Montfort *TD: #102-103*

There is another category of false devotees of our Lady – hypocritical ones. These hide their sins and evil habits under the mantle of the Blessed Virgin so as to appear to their fellow men different from what they are.

Then there are the self-interested devotees who turn to her only to win a court-case, to escape some danger, to be cured of some ailment or to have some similar need satisfied. Except when in need they never think of her. Such people are acceptable neither to God nor to his Mother.

Question

What is the image of yourself that you present to the world? What is the reality within you?

Resolution

It is very common to do what is good so that others might see and notice us and not for a truly holy motivation. Look for an opportunity to be generous in a hidden way and do it.

Prayer: JESUS LIVING IN MARY (PG. 13)

Night Prayer: SUB TUUM (PG. 18)

DAY SEVEN
The Flesh is Opposed to the Spirit

Prayer: INVOCATION OF THE HOLY SPIRIT (PG. 12)

Scripture   *Galatians 5: 16-21*

But I say, walk by the Spirit, and do not gratify the desires of the flesh. For the desires of the flesh are against the Spirit, and the desires of the Spirit are against the flesh; for these are opposed to each other, to prevent you from doing what you would. But if you are led by the Spirit you are not under the law. Now the works of the flesh are plain: immorality, impurity, licentiousness, idolatry, sorcery, enmity, strife, jealousy, anger, selfishness, dissensions, party spirit, envy, drunkenness, carousing, and the like. I warn you, as I warned you before, that those who do such things shall not inherit the kingdom of God.

St. Louis de Montfort   *LEW: #81*

The wisdom of the flesh is the love of pleasure. This is the wisdom shown by the worldly-wise who seek only the satisfaction of the senses. They want to have a good time. They shun anything that might prove unpleasant or mortifying for the body, such as fasting and other austerities. Usually they think only of eating, drinking, playing, laughing, enjoying life and having a good time. They must always be comfortable and insist on having entertaining pastimes, the best of food and good company.

Question

Everyone experiences temptations of the flesh. What manner of this form of temptation is most powerful in your life?

Resolution

Deny one of your sensual appetites today.

Prayer: JESUS LIVING IN MARY (PG. 13)

Night Prayer: SUB TUUM (PG. 18)

DAY EIGHT
The World loves the Darkness

Prayer: INVOCATION OF THE HOLY SPIRIT (PG. 12)

Scripture   *John 3: 19-21*

And this is the judgment, that the light has come into the world, and men loved darkness rather than light, because their deeds were evil. For everyone who does evil hates the light, and does not come to the light, lest his deeds should be exposed. But he who does what is true comes to the light, that it may be clearly seen that their deeds have been wrought in God.

St. Louis de Montfort   *LEW: #82*

Diabolical wisdom is the love of esteem and honors. This is the wisdom of the worldly-wise who, secretly of course, long for distinctions, honors, dignities and high offices. They strive to be seen, esteemed, praised and applauded by men. In their studies, their work, their words and actions, all they want is the esteem and praise of men, to be reputed as devout or learned people, as great leaders, eminent lawyers, men of great and distinguished merit or deserving of high consideration. They cannot bear insult or blame and so they hide their shortcomings and parade their better qualities.

Resolution

Make an examination of conscience. Decide when you will celebrate the sacrament of reconciliation during the preparation period. If you cannot celebrate this sacrament, seek out an opportunity to speak with a priest concerning the state of your spiritual life.

Prayer: JESUS LIVING IN MARY (PG. 13)

Night Prayer: SUB TUUM (PG. 18)

DAY NINE
Lay Aside the Works of Darkness

Prayer: INVOCATION OF THE HOLY SPIRIT (PG. 12)

Scripture   *Romans 13: 11-14*

Besides this, you know what hour it is, how it is full time now for you to wake from sleep. For salvation is nearer to us now than when we first believed; the night is far gone, the day is at hand. Let us then cast off the works of darkness and put on the armor of light; let us conduct ourselves becomingly as in the day, not in reveling and drunkenness, not in debauchery and licentiousness, not in quarreling and jealousy. But put on the Lord Jesus Christ, and make no provision for the flesh, to gratify its desires.

St. Louis de Montfort   *TD: #108*

True devotion to Mary is holy. That is, it leads us to avoid sin and to imitate the virtues of Mary. Her ten principal virtues are: deep humility, lively faith, blind obedience, unceasing prayer, constant self-denial, surpassing purity, ardent love, heroic patience, angelic kindness and heavenly wisdom.

Resolution

Choose one of the Blessed Virgin's virtues and practice it throughout the day.

Prayer: JESUS LIVING IN MARY (PG. 13)

Night Prayer: SUB TUUM (PG. 18)

DAY TEN
False Blessedness

Prayer: INVOCATION OF THE HOLY SPIRIT (PG. 12)

Scripture   *Luke 12:16-21*

Then he told them a parable, saying, "The land of a rich man brought forth plentifully; and he thought to himself, 'What shall I do, for I have nowhere to store my crops?' And he said, 'I will do this: I will pull down my barns, and build larger ones; and there I will store all my grain and my goods. And I will say to my soul, 'Soul, you have ample goods laid up for many years; take your ease, eat, drink, be merry.' But God said to him, 'Fool! This night your soul is required of you; and the things you have prepared, whose will they be?' So is he who lays up treasures for himself, and is not rich toward God."

St. Louis de Montfort   *TD: #97-98*

Presumptuous devotees are sinners who give full reign to their passions or their love of the world, and who, under the fair name of Christian and servant of our Lady, conceal pride, avarice, lust, drunkenness, anger, swearing, slandering, injustice and other vices. They sleep peacefully in their wicked habits, without making any great effort to correct them, believing that their devotion to our Lady gives them this sort of liberty. They convince themselves that God will forgive them, that they will not die without confession, that they will not be lost for all eternity...

When you tell them that such a devotion is only an illusion of the devil and a dangerous presumption which may well ruin them, they refuse to believe you. God is good and merciful, they reply, and he has not made us to damn us. No man is without sin. We will not die without confession and a good act of contrition at death is all that is needed. Moreover, they say they have devotion to Our Lady...

Nothing in our Christian religion is so deserving of condemnation as this diabolical presumption.

Question

Is there a persistent sin or vice in your life that you are not fighting against? Why have you made your peace with this?

Prayer: JESUS LIVING IN MARY (PG. 13)

Night Prayer: SUB TUUM (PG. 18)

DAY ELEVEN
True and False Religion

Prayer: INVOCATION OF THE HOLY SPIRIT (PG. 12)

Scripture   *James 1: 21-27*

Therefore put away all filthiness and rank growth of wickedness and receive with meekness the implanted word which is able to save your souls. But be doers of the word, and not hearers only, deceiving yourselves. For if any one is a hearer of the word and not a doer, he is like a man who observes his natural face in a mirror; for he observes himself and goes away and at once forgets what he was like. But he who looks into the perfect law, the law of liberty, and perseveres, being no hearer that forgets but a doer who acts, he shall be blessed in his doing. If anyone thinks he is religious, but does not bridle his tongue but deceives his heart, this man's religion is vain. Religion that is pure and undefiled before God and the Father is this: to visit orphans and widows in their affliction, and to keep oneself unstained from the world.

St. Louis de Montfort   *TD: #101*

Inconstant devotees are those whose devotion to our Lady is practiced in fits and starts. Sometimes they are fervent and sometimes they are lukewarm. Sometimes they appear ready to do anything to please our Lady, and then shortly afterwards they have completely changed. They start by embracing every devotion to our Lady. They join her confraternities, but they do not faithfully observe the rules. They are as changeable as the moon, and like the moon Mary puts them under her feet. Because of their fickleness they are unworthy to be included among the servants of the Virgin because faithfulness and constancy are the hallmarks of Mary's servants. It is better not to burden ourselves with a multitude of prayers and pious practices but rather adopt only a few and perform them with love and perseverance in spite of opposition from the devil and the world and the flesh.

Resolution

Faithfulness in simple things is much more valuable than inconstant activity in greater things. If you are not attending Mass every Sunday, make the decision to do so. If you are doing so faithfully, ask yourself how you might improve your participation in the liturgy and do it.

Prayer: JESUS LIVING IN MARY (PG. 13)

Night Prayer: SUB TUUM (PG. 18)

DAY TWELVE
Consecration in the Truth

Prayer: INVOCATION OF THE HOLY SPIRIT (PG. 12)

Scripture   *John 17:14-19*

I have given them your word; and the world has hated them because they are not of the world, even as I am not of the world. I do not pray that you should take them out of the world, but that you should keep them from the evil one. They are not of the world, even as I am not of the world. Sanctify them in the truth; your word is truth. As you sent me into the world, so I have sent them into the world. And for their sake I consecrate myself, that they also may be consecrated in truth.

St. Louis de Montfort   *TD: #59*

Lastly, we know they will be true disciples of Jesus Christ, imitating his poverty, his humility, his contempt of the world and his love. They will point out the narrow way to God in the pure truth of the holy Gospel and not according to the maxims of the world. Their hearts will not be troubled, nor will they show favor to anyone; they will not spare or heed or fear any man, however powerful he may be. They will have the two-edged sword of the Word of God in their mouths and the blood-stained standard of the Cross on their shoulders. They will carry the crucifix in their right hand and the rosary in their left, and the holy names of Jesus and Mary in their heart. The simplicity and self-sacrifice of Jesus will be reflected in their whole behavior.

41

Question

Jesus tells us that we have the mission of being light for the world, not slaves of the world. In your daily life, how can you more effectively be light for others?

Prayer: JESUS LIVING IN MARY (PG. 13)

Night Prayer: SUB TUUM (PG. 18)
SUB AVE MARIS STELLA (PG. 43)

These twelve days faithfully observed have borne fruit. Consider for a few moments what you have learned about yourself and the ways that the spirit of the world has influenced you. Consider for a few moments how difficult, and how necessary, it is to overcome this spirit. Consider for a few moments how you have grown in your resolve to overcome, by the grace of God, the spirit of the world. Before moving forward into the next period prayerfully ask Our Lady to aid and sustain you.

AVE MARIS STELLA

Hail, O Star of the ocean,
God's own Mother blest,
ever sinless Virgin,
gate of heavenly rest.
Taking that sweet Ave,
which from Gabriel came,
peace confirm within us,
changing Eva's name.
Break the sinners' fetters,
make our blindness day,
Chase all evils from us,
for all blessings pray.
Show thyself a Mother,
may the Word divine
born for us thine Infant
hear our prayers through thine.
Virgin all excelling,
mildest of the mild,
free from guilt preserve us
meek and undefiled.
Keep our life all spotless,
make our way secure
till we find in Jesus,
joy for evermore.
Praise to God the Father,
honor to the Son,
in the Holy Spirit,
be the glory one.
Amen.

Statue of St. Louis de Montfort from the
Montfortian Retreat House in Fatima, Portugal.

TO BE FILLED WITH
THE SPIRIT OF JESUS CHRIST

———

*They should then spend three weeks
imbuing themselves with the spirit of Jesus
through the Most Blessed Virgin.*

WEEK ONE
KNOWLEDGE OF SELF

...

Let them perform all their actions
in a spirit of humility.

THE GRACE OF SELF-KNOWLEDGE

FR. DE MONTFORT WRITES THAT DURING THIS WEEK THOSE WHO seek to be filled with the spirit of Jesus "should offer up all their prayers and acts of devotion to acquire knowledge of themselves and sorrow for their sins." Having struggled against the spirit of the world for twelve days we come to the realization that the spirit of the world is not only self-centered, it is self-deceiving. In turning away from the Lord, the worldly spirit founds its life upon the lie of its false and complacent self-sufficiency and seeks to order all things in terms of its self-indulgence. In refusing to know the Lord the worldly spirit is incapable of knowing the truth about itself. This is why the step of self-knowledge follows necessarily upon a turning away from the spirit of the world and also why the first twelve days are so necessary for this process. Only now can we begin to come to terms with the truth of ourselves. True self-knowledge is not a thing that is easily obtained, nor can it be obtained solely through our own efforts. It is a gift from God, a grace so important that Fr. de Montfort calls it "that great grace which is the foundation of all others."

Humility is the key to this step. Coming to terms with who we truly are requires that we recognize, as we will endeavor to do on the second day of this week, that none of us is the owner and master of his life. Whether one is willing to admit so or not does not change the fundamental reality that each of us belongs to Almighty God and that it is to God that we are accountable for the life we have been given. Baptized into the dying and rising of Jesus, given a share in his life, the Christian belongs more fully and intimately to the Almighty than any other. This too is the reality of our lives. There is a fundamental greatness about us that Fr. de Montfort would have us recognize, a greatness that has nothing to do with our talents or merits or accomplishments but that is a Divine gift. Recognizing this gift in all of its greatness, however, should humble us with the additional recognition of how easily and often we allow the power of sin to rob us of our full dignity. St. Louis de Montfort would have us beg the Lord and his Holy Spirit to teach us three things about ourselves this week:

• The life of holiness to which we are called as a result of our belonging completely to Jesus Christ.

• The extent to which we are unable, due to sinfulness, weakness, and inconstancy, to fully and authentically live this life of holiness by our own efforts.

• That we need help to live the life of grace.

For Night Prayer over these seven days one is asked to simply pause a few moments in prayerful reflection that recalls the theme of the day and the fruits of one's meditation upon it. One then follows Fr. de Montfort's instruction that "they will turn to our Blessed Lady and beg her to obtain for them that great grace which is the foundation of all others, the grace of self-knowledge." This is done by praying with confidence the *Memorare* of St. Bernard of Clairvaux. The *Memorare* was one of St. Louis de Montfort's favorite prayers and he used it as a model in the writing of his own prayers to Our Lady. While praying the *Memorare* each night it is important to allow the spirit of this beautiful invocation of the Blessed Mother's aid to penetrate our hearts and instruct us as it did Fr. de Montfort.

The Memorare

Remember,
O most gracious Virgin Mary,
that never was it known that anyone
who fled to your protection,
implored your help or
sought your intercession
was left unaided.

Inspired by this confidence,
I fly unto you,
O Virgin of virgins, my mother;
to thee do I come,
before thee I stand,
sinful and sorrowful.

O Mother of the Word Incarnate,
despise not my petitions,
but in your mercy hear and answer me.
Amen.

At the beginning of this week and before moving to the first day's spiritual exercises, it is important to hear once again the words of Fr. de Montfort who reminds us of the greatness of life to which we are called by virtue of our baptism into Jesus Christ: "It is certain that growth in holiness is your vocation." Rather than the great multitude of those who have made easy compromise with or surrendered to the false values of the world, St. Louis de Montfort would have us look to that great cloud of witnesses who have been transformed by the power of grace into living testimonies of the love of God in Jesus Christ. One's first step along the way of self-knowledge is, therefore, to invoke the aid and intercession of the Communion of Saints that they support us during this week with their prayer. This is done by praying the *Litany of the Saints*. While one is certainly free to make the Litany part of his daily prayer over these seven days, it is only necessary to pray it on the first.

Upon completing the exercises for the seventh day, one places the fruits of this time in the hands of the Blessed Virgin by praying the *Ave Maris Stella*.

LITANY OF THE SAINTS

If one has an image of his patron saint, it is recommended to pray this litany before that image. One should also make it a point to include his patron saint among the invocations, adding the name after the invocation of Saint Maximilian Kolbe.

Lord, have mercy	Lord, have mercy
Christ, have mercy	Christ, have mercy
Lord, have mercy	Lord, have mercy

Holy Mary, Mother of God,	pray for us
Saint Michael,	pray for us
Holy angels of God,	pray for us
Saint John the Baptist,	pray for us
Saint Joseph,	pray for us
Saint Peter and Saint Paul,	pray for us
Saint Andrew,	pray for us
Saint John,	pray for us
Saint Mary Magdalene,	pray for us
Saint Stephen,	pray for us

Saint Ignatius of Antioch,	pray for us
Saint Lawrence,	pray for us
Saint Perpetua and Saint Felicity,	pray for us
Saint Agnes,	pray for us
Saint Gregory,	pray for us
Saint Augustine,	pray for us
Saint Basil,	pray for us
Saint Martin,	pray for us
Saint Benedict,	pray for us
Saint Francis and Saint Dominic,	pray for us

Saint Francis Xavier,	pray for us
Saint John Vianney,	pray for us
Saint Catherine,	pray for us
Saint Teresa of Jesus,	pray for us
Saint Bernard of Clairvaux,	pray for us
Saint Thomas Aquinas,	pray for us
Saint Vincent Ferrer,	pray for us
Saint Juan Diego,	pray for us
Saint John Eudes	pray for us
Saint Louis Marie de Montfort,	pray for us
Saint Bernadette,	pray for us
Saint Maximilian Kolbe,	pray for us
All holy men and women,	pray for us
Lord, be merciful,	Lord, deliver us, we pray
From all evil,	Lord, deliver us, we pray
From every sin,	Lord, deliver us, we pray
From everlasting death,	Lord, deliver us, we pray
By your coming as man,	Lord, deliver us, we pray
By your death and rising to new life,	Lord, deliver us, we pray
By your gift of the Holy Spirit,	Lord, deliver us, we pray
Be merciful to us sinners,	Lord, we ask you, hear our prayer
Guide and protect your holy Church,	Lord, we ask you, hear our prayer
Keep the pope and all the clergy in faithful service to your Church,	Lord, we ask you, hear our prayer

Bring all peoples together
  in trust and peace,   Lord, we ask you,
                                      hear our prayer

Strengthen us in your service,   Lord, we ask you,
                                      hear our prayer

Jesus, Son of the living God,   Lord, we ask you,
                                      hear our prayer

Christ, hear us   Christ, hear us
Christ, graciously hear us   Christ, graciously hear us

God of our ancestors who set their hearts on you,
of those who fell asleep in peace,
and of those who won the martyrs' violent crown:
we are surrounded by these witnesses
as by clouds of fragrant incense.
In this age we would be counted
in this communion of all the saints;
keep us always in their good and blessed company.
In their midst we make every prayer
through Christ who is our Lord for ever and ever.
Amen.

DAY ONE
Baptized into the Dying and Rising of Christ

Prayer: INVOCATION OF THE HOLY SPIRIT (PG. 12)

Scripture   *Romans 6: 3-11*

Do you not know that all of us who have been baptized into Christ Jesus were baptized into his death? We were buried therefore with him by baptism into death, so that as Christ was raised from the dead by the glory of the Father, we too might walk in newness of life. For if we have been united with him in a death like his, we shall certainly be united with him in a resurrection like his. We know that our old self was crucified with him so that the sinful body might be destroyed, and we might no longer be enslaved to sin. For he who has died is freed from sin. But if we have died with Christ, we believe that we shall also live with him. For we know that Christ being raised from the dead will never die again; death no longer has dominion over him. The death he died he died to sin, once for all, but the life he lives he lives to God. So you also must consider yourselves dead to sin and alive to God in Christ Jesus.

St. Louis de Montfort   *TD: #127*

"Men," says St. Thomas, "vow in baptism to renounce the devil and all his seductions". "This vow," says St. Augustine, "is the greatest and the most indispensable of all vows". Canon law experts say the same thing: "The vow we make at baptism is the most important of all vows". But does anyone keep this great vow? Does anyone fulfill the promises of baptism faithfully? Is it not true that nearly all Christians prove unfaithful to the promises made to Jesus in baptism? Where does this universal failure come from, if not from man's habitual forgetfulness of the promises and responsibilities of baptism and from the fact that scarcely anyone makes a personal ratification of the contract made with God through his sponsors?

Question

What is the vow we make in baptism? Are you conscious in your daily living of the importance of keeping this great promise? In your life, do you have difficulty in being faithful to your commitments or in keeping the promises you make? Does making and keeping a permanent commitment frighten you?

Prayer: JESUS LIVING IN MARY (PG. 13)

Night Prayer: MEMORARE (PG. 49)

DAY TWO
I am not The Owner of My Life

Prayer: INVOCATION OF THE HOLY SPIRIT (PG. 12)

Scripture   *Romans 7: 4-6*

Likewise, my brethren, you have died to the law through the body of Christ, so that you may belong to another, to him who has been raised from the dead in order that we may bear fruit for God. While we were living in the flesh, our sinful passions, aroused by the law, were at work in our members to bear fruit for death. But now we are discharged from the law, dead to that which held us captive, so that we serve not under the old written code but in the new life of the Spirit.

St. Louis de Montfort   *TD: #68*

From what Jesus Christ is in regard to us we must conclude, as St. Paul says, that we belong not to ourselves but entirely to him as his members and his slaves, for he has bought us at an infinite price – the shedding of his Precious Blood. Before baptism, we belonged to the devil as slaves, but baptism made us in very truth slaves of Jesus. We must therefore live, work and die for the sole purpose of bringing forth fruit for him, glorifying him in our body and letting him reign in our soul. We are his conquest, the people he has won, his heritage.

Question

It is one thing to belong to Christ, and quite another to submit one's will and desires to him. Do my sins continue to dominate me?

Do I have an affection for or attachment to a particular sin that I need to set aside?

Prayer: JESUS LIVING IN MARY (PG. 13)

Night Prayer: MEMORARE (PG. 49)

DAY THREE
I am a Sinner

Prayer: INVOCATION OF THE HOLY SPIRIT (PG. 12)

Scripture   *1 John 1: 8-10*

If we say we have no sin, we deceive ourselves, and the truth is not in us. If we confess our sins, he is faithful and just, and will forgive our sins and cleanse us from all unrighteousness. If we say we have not sinned, we make him a liar, and his word is not in us.

St. Louis de Montfort   *TD: #99-100*

I admit to be truly devoted to our Lady it is not absolutely necessary to be so holy as to avoid all sin, although this is desirable. But at least it is necessary (note what I am going to say) (i) to be genuinely determined to avoid at least all mortal sin, which outrages the Mother as well as the Son; (ii) to practice great self-restraint in order to avoid sin; (iii) to join her confraternities, say the rosary or other prayers, fast on Saturdays and so on.

Such means are surprisingly effective in converting even the most hardened sinner. Should you be such a sinner, with one foot in the abyss, I advise you to do as I have said. But there is an essential condition. You must perform these good works solely to obtain from God, through the intercession of our Lady, the grace to regret your sins, obtain pardon for them and overcome your evil habits, and not to live complacently in the state of sin, disregarding the warning voice of conscience, the example of our Lord and the saints and the teaching of the holy gospel.

Question

Everyone has his or her bad habits and vices. What are yours?

Resolution

Make a firm decision to overcome one of your bad habits. Do not continue with the process until you have begun to act on this decision.

Prayer: JESUS LIVING IN MARY (PG. 13)

Night Prayer: MEMORARE (PG. 49)

DAY FOUR
The Tree is known by its Fruit

Prayer: INVOCATION OF THE HOLY SPIRIT (PG. 12)

Scripture   *Luke 6: 43-45*

For no good tree bears bad fruit, nor again does a bad tree bear good fruit; for each tree is known by its own fruit. For figs are not gathered from thorns, nor are grapes picked from a bramble bush. The good man out of the good treasure of his heart produces good, and the evil man out of his evil treasure produces evil; for out of the abundance of the heart his mouth speaks.

St. Louis de Montfort   *TD: #78*

Our best actions are usually tainted and spoiled by the evil that is rooted in us. When pure, clear water is poured into a foul-smelling jug, or wine into an unwashed cask that previously contained another wine, the clear water and the good wine are tainted and readily acquire an unpleasant odor. In the same way when God pours into our soul, infected by original and actual sin, the heavenly waters of his grace and the delicious wines of his love, his gifts are usually spoiled and tainted by the evil sediment left in us by sin. Our actions, even those of the highest virtue, show the effects of it. It is therefore of the utmost importance that, in seeking the perfection that can only be attained by union with Jesus, we rid ourselves of all that is evil in us.

Question

The things you say, especially those said when you are in private or when you are frustrated, what do they indicate about the state of your heart?

Prayer: JESUS LIVING IN MARY (PG. 13)

Night Prayer: MEMORARE (PG. 49)

DAY FIVE
I am Weak

Prayer: INVOCATION OF THE HOLY SPIRIT (PG. 12)

Scripture   *Romans 7: 21-25*

So I find it to be a law that when I want to do right, evil lies close at hand. For I delight in the law of God, in my inmost self, but I see in my members another law at war with the law of my mind and making me captive to the law of sin which dwells in my members. Wretched man that I am! Who will deliver me from this body of death? Thanks be to God through Jesus Christ our Lord! So then, I of myself serve the law of God with my mind, but with my flesh I serve the law of sin.

St. Louis de Montfort   *TD: #87*

It is very difficult, considering our weakness and frailty, to keep the graces and treasures we have received from God. We carry this treasure, which is worth more than heaven and earth, in fragile vessels, that is, in a corruptible body and in a weak and wavering soul which requires very little to depress and disturb it.

Question

Consider your personal history – how many occasions of grace and moments of blessing have you lost over the course of your life? How many times have sin or inconstancy robbed you of blessing?

Prayer: JESUS LIVING IN MARY (PG. 13)

Night Prayer: MEMORARE (PG. 49)

Day Six
I must Humble myself before the Lord

Prayer: INVOCATION OF THE HOLY SPIRIT (PG. 12)

Scripture   *Luke 18: 9-14*

He also told this parable to some who trusted in themselves that they were righteous and despised others: "Two men went up into the temple to pray, one a Pharisee and the other a tax collector. The Pharisee stood and prayed thus with himself, 'God, I thank thee that I am not like other men, extortioners, unjust, adulterers, or even like this tax collector. I fast twice a week, I give tithes of all that I get.' But the tax collector, standing far off, would not even lift up his eyes to heaven, but beat his breast, saying, 'God, be merciful to me a sinner!' I tell you, this man went down to his house justified rather than the other; for every one who exalts himself will be humbled, but he who humbles himself will be exalted."

St. Louis de Montfort   *SM: #36*

In going to Jesus through Mary, we are really paying honor to our Lord, for we are showing that, because of our sins, we are unworthy to approach his infinite holiness directly on our own. We are showing that we need Mary, his holy Mother, to be our advocate and media-trix with him who is our Mediator. We are going to Jesus as Mediator and Brother, and at the same time humbling ourselves before him who is our God and our Judge. In short we are practicing humility, something which always gladdens the heart of God.

Question

Why is a genuine humility such an important virtue for the spiritual life?

Resolution

As you pray today, allow your recognition of your sinfulness and your weakness to lead you to seek out the intercession of Mary. Make it a point to approach the Lord in her company.

Prayer: JESUS LIVING IN MARY (PG. 13)

Night Prayer: MEMORARE (PG. 49)

DAY SEVEN
I must deny Myself

Prayer: INVOCATION OF THE HOLY SPIRIT (PG. 12)

Scripture   *Mark 8: 34-37*

And he called to him the multitude with his disciples, and said to them, "If any man would come after me, let him deny himself and take up his cross and follow me. For whoever would save his life will lose it; and whoever loses his life for my sake and the gospel's will save it. For what does it profit a man, to gain the whole world and forfeit his life? For what can a man give in return for his life?"

St. Louis de Montfort   *TD: #81*

In order to empty ourselves of self, we must die daily to ourselves. This involves our renouncing what the powers of the soul and the senses of the body incline us to do. We must see as if we did not see, hear as if we did not hear and use the things of the world as if we did not use them. This is what St. Paul calls *dying daily*. Unless the grain of wheat falls to the ground and dies, it remains only a single grain and does not bear any good fruit. If we do not die to self and if our holiest devotions do not lead us to this necessary and fruitful death, we shall not bear fruit of any worth and our devotions will cease to be profitable. All our good works will be tainted by self-love and self-will so that our greatest sacrifices and our best actions will be unacceptable to God. Consequently when we come to die we shall find ourselves devoid of virtue and merit and discover that we do not possess even one spark of that pure love which God shares only with those who have died to themselves and whose life is hidden with Jesus Christ in him.

Question

To die to oneself is not simply to renounce sin. It is also to recognize that even our very best inclinations and capacities need to be purified. This death is not the destruction of ourselves, but the transformation of our fragility and limitation into the strength and power of God. This change is not possible without the Cross. Where do you encounter the Cross in your life? Do you embrace and carry this Cross with a faithful heart or do you seek out opportunities to set it aside?

Prayer: JESUS LIVING IN MARY (PG. 13)

Night Prayer: MEMORARE (PG. 49)
AVE MARIS STELLA (PG. 67)

These seven days faithfully observed have borne fruit. Consider for a few moments what you have learned about who you truly are. Consider for a few moments the slavery to sin which prevents you from living in the full freedom of the children of God. Consider how you have deepened in desire to repent and throw off the chains of this sinfulness. Consider how difficult, yet how necessary, this will be. Before moving forward into the next period, prayerfully ask Our Lady to aid and sustain you.

AVE MARIS STELLA

Hail, O Star of the ocean,
God's own Mother blest,
ever sinless Virgin,
gate of heavenly rest.
Taking that sweet Ave,
which from Gabriel came,
peace confirm within us,
changing Eva's name.
Break the sinners' fetters,
make our blindness day,
Chase all evils from us,
for all blessings pray.
Show thyself a Mother,
may the Word divine
born for us thine Infant
hear our prayers through thine.
Virgin all excelling,
mildest of the mild,
free from guilt preserve us
meek and undefiled.
Keep our life all spotless,
make our way secure
till we find in Jesus,
joy for evermore.
Praise to God the Father,
honor to the Son,
in the Holy Spirit,
be the glory one.
Amen.

WEEK TWO
KNOWLEDGE OF MARY

...

*Mary must be known
and openly revealed by the Holy Spirit
so that Jesus may be known
and loved through her.*

— St. Louis de Montfort

A SECRET WHOSE NAME IS MARY

KNOWLEDGE OF MARY IS A GIFT SO GREAT THAT IT IS NOTHING less than a privileged grace that one receives from the hand of the Almighty himself. Fr. de Montfort places great emphasis on this in speaking of Our Lady: "Mary is the supreme masterpiece of Almighty God and he has reserved the knowledge and possession of her for himself ...She is the sanctuary and resting place of the Blessed Trinity... No creature, however pure, may enter there without being specially privileged." (TD #5) Mary is the secret treasure and prized possession of the Most High. A secret that is so valuable, a possession that is so greatly treasured, is something that one would only consider sharing with a truly intimate, and trusted, friend. The invitation to true knowledge, knowledge that is deeply personal, of Our Lady is, therefore, nothing less than an invitation to an intimate sharing, a sign of a deep and privileged friendship, with the Lord of all glory, the Maker of heaven and earth. It is vital that we recognize that this step forward in the preparation process is in itself the beginning of something truly great within our lives. It is now time to build upon the foundational grace of self-knowledge, and what is to be built upon this foundation is something of infinite value, a vital and deeply personal relationship with Mary. Knowledge of Mary is established upon the foundation of knowledge of oneself and it is the work of the same Holy Spirit, who illumines us and reveals to us the reality of ourselves, that allows us access to that marvelous secret of the Most High whose name is Mary.

It is precisely what we have learned about ourselves by the light of the Holy Spirit that will be our point of contact for entering into a truly personal relationship with Our Lady. We have discovered that without the grace of God to aid us and to sustain us, we cannot make more than tentative, awkward and inconstant movements toward genuine spiritual growth. Mary is that one who is truly Full of Grace, not only for herself, but marvelously for us as well. Therefore we will begin this week by opening our need for grace to the kindness and generosity of Our Lady. We are sinners and our struggles against temptation are constant and often end badly. Therefore we will turn to Our Lady in the flesh and blood of our struggle against all those things that would seduce us away from the path of life. We are weak and have great difficulty in holding on to the blessings we have received. Our intentions are impure and even our best attempts at generosity are colored by a hidden and prideful selfishness. Our Lady is the treasury of God himself and her intentions are always pure. Therefore we will learn how to place, with great confidence, all that is best about our lives into her care, secure that its value will never be diminished and will, in fact, only be purified and increased through her stewardship. In doing all of this we will come to experience Mary as a Mother and a Queen who is intimately, directly and effectively involved in our lives - a deeply personal knowledge. This personal knowledge of her does not rest upon our goodness, nor upon our purity, nor upon our worthiness, but upon our need for her and a humble willingness to turn to her in trust, and upon the generosity of the Lord who grants us the grace of knowing her. And most marvelously, in turning to Our Lady and entrusting ourselves into her care we will find that we have already begun to act according to the spirit of Jesus Christ, the first to have trusted himself into the care of Our Lady.

Our prayer will change during this week. The patterns of prayer that we begin during these days are vital movements of St. Louis de

Montfort's spirituality of consecration, movements that we will carry forward through the remainder of the preparation process and movements that will prove to be a permanent part of our spiritual lives as we live the Total Consecration which we are preparing to make. Change to the way we pray is always a bit disconcerting and it is natural to feel a bit of awkwardness at the beginning. It is important to recognize that what we do here is take the first small steps toward cultivating habits of the heart in our relationship with Mary, habits which will grow deeper with time and that in time will yield up the fruits of a deep confidence in her Maternal intercession and care for us. Learning to consistently turn to Our Lady in our need for grace, entrusting to her care all that is most important in our lives, and invoking her intercession in time of temptation are all necessary elements of the spirituality of consecration.

Night Prayer during these seven days takes on an additional fullness. One is asked not to meditate on Our Lady, but to turn to her with confidence. In turning to her each night, one is asked to consider where there is a need for grace in his life, to examine his conscience and identify the strongest and most persistent temptations, and to recognize the ways in which the goodness of God has touched his life that day. In all of this we turn to Mary with confident words with which St. Louis de Montfort concludes one of his formulae for saying the Holy Rosary. *(See next page)*

St. Louis de Montfort's Rosary Prayer

Hail Mary, well-beloved daughter of the eternal Father,
admirable Mother of the Son,
most faithful spouse of the Holy Spirit,
august Temple of the most holy Trinity.
Hail, sovereign Princess,
to whom all is subject in Heaven and on earth.
Hail, sure Refuge of sinners,
Our Lady of Mercy who has never rejected anyone,
all sinful that I am, I cast myself at your feet,
and I ask you to obtain for me from the good Jesus, your dear Son,
contrition and pardon for all of my sins along with divine wisdom.

I consecrate myself entirely to you along with all that I have.
I take you today for my Mother and my Mistress;
treat me then as the last of your children
and the most obedient of your servants:
Listen, my Princess, listen to the sighs of a heart
that desires to love you and to serve you faithfully.
Let it not be said that of all of those who have had recourse to you,
that I have been the first to be abandoned!

O my hope! O my life!
O my faithful and immaculate Virgin Mary!
graciously hear me, defend me, nourish me,
instruct me, save me.
Amen.

At the beginning of this week and before moving to the first day's spiritual exercises, we step out in confidence and invoke Our Lady's intercession by praying the *Litany of Loreto (pg. 74)*. Even as we do this, we begin to grow in knowledge of her not by simply reading a list of her titles but by naming her in the many ways she has been a source of comfort, of aid, and of refuge to all of those who have turned to her for two millennia. In doing this, we remind ourselves of just how great a gift, how remarkable a privilege it is that the Almighty share with us his prized possession and secret treasure whose name is Mary. While one is certainly free to make the Litany part of his daily prayer over these seven days, it is only necessary to pray it on the first.

Upon completing the exercises for the seventh day, one places the fruits of this time in the hands of the Blessed Virgin by praying the Holy Rosary and concluding with the *Ave Maris Stella*.

It would be very desirable to make the praying of the Holy Rosary a part of one's daily prayer this week. Even if one does not have the time to pray it each day, it should be prayed on the seventh day. A method of saying the rosary according to St. Louis de Montfort is included in the Appendix.

LITANY OF LORETO

It is recommended to pray this Litany before an image of Our Lady.

Lord, have mercy	Lord, have mercy
Christ, have mercy	Christ, have mercy
Lord, have mercy	Lord, have mercy
God our Father in heaven	have mercy on us
God the Son, Redeemer of the world	have mercy on us
God the Holy Spirit	have mercy on us
Holy Trinity, one God	have mercy on us
Holy Mary	pray for us
Holy Mother of God	pray for us
Most honored of virgins	pray for us
Mother of Christ	pray for us
Mother of the Church	pray for us
Mother of divine grace	pray for us
Mother most pure	pray for us
Mother of chaste love	pray for us
Mother and virgin	pray for us
Sinless Mother	pray for us
Dearest of mothers	pray for us
Model of motherhood	pray for us
Mother of good counsel	pray for us
Mother of our Creator	pray for us
Mother of our Savior	pray for us
Virgin most wise	pray for us
Virgin rightly praised	pray for us
Virgin rightly renowned	pray for us

Virgin most powerful	pray for us
Virgin gentle in mercy	pray for us
Faithful Virgin	pray for us
Mirror of justice	pray for us
Throne of wisdom	pray for us
Cause of our joy	pray for us
Shrine of the Spirit	pray for us
Glory of Israel	pray for us
Vessel of selfless devotion	pray for us
Mystical Rose	pray for us
Tower of David	pray for us
Tower of ivory	pray for us
House of gold	pray for us
Ark of the covenant	pray for us
Gate of heaven	pray for us
Morning Star	pray for us
Health of the sick	pray for us
Refuge of sinners	pray for us
Comfort of the troubled	pray for us
Help of Christians	pray for us
Queen of angels	pray for us
Queen of patriarchs and prophets	pray for us
Queen of apostles and martyrs	pray for us
Queen of confessors and virgins	pray for us
Queen of all saints	pray for us
Queen conceived without original sin	pray for us
Queen assumed into heaven	pray for us
Queen of the rosary	pray for us
Queen of families	pray for us
Queen of peace	pray for us

Lamb of God,
> you take away the sins of the world   have mercy on us

Lamb of God,
> you take away the sins of the world   have mercy on us

Lamb of God,
> you take away the sins of the world   have mercy on us

Pray for us, holy Mother of God.
That we may become worthy of the promises of Christ.

Eternal God,
let your people enjoy constant health in mind and body.
Through the intercession of the Virgin Mary
free us from the sorrows of this life
and lead us to happiness in the life to come.
Grant this through Christ our Lord.
Amen.

DAY ONE
Mary Full of Grace

Prayer: INVOCATION OF THE HOLY SPIRIT (PG. 12)

Scripture   *1 Corinthians 1: 4-8*

I give thanks to God always for you because of the grace of God which was given you in Christ Jesus, that in every way you were enriched in him with all speech and all knowledge - even as the testimony to Christ was confirmed among you - so that you are not lacking in any spiritual gift, as you wait for the revealing of our Lord Jesus Christ; who will sustain you to the end, guiltless in the day of our Lord Jesus Christ.

St. Louis de Montfort   *TD: #44*

Mary alone found grace before God without the help of any other creature. All those who have since found grace before God have found it only through her. She was full of grace when she was greeted by the Archangel Gabriel and was filled with grace to overflowing by the Holy Spirit when he so mysteriously overshadowed her. From day to day, from moment to moment, she increased so much this two-fold plenitude that she attained an immense and inconceivable degree of grace. So much so that the Almighty made her the sole custodian of his treasures and the sole dispenser of his graces. She can ennoble, exalt and enrich all she chooses. She can lead them along the narrow path to heaven and guide them through the narrow gate of life. She can give a royal throne, scepter and crown to whom she wishes. Jesus is always and everywhere the fruit and Son of Mary and Mary is everywhere the genuine tree that bears the Fruit of life, the true Mother who bears that Son.

77

Question

In your life, where do you experience the greatest need for the grace of God?

Resolution

In your prayer today place this aspect of your life in the hands of Mary and ask her to obtain from her Son the grace that you need. Continue to pray in this way each day.

Prayer: JESUS LIVING IN MARY (PG. 13)

Night Prayer: ST. LOUIS DE MONTFORT'S ROSARY PRAYER (PG. 72)

DAY TWO
Mary is the Powerful enemy of satan

Prayer: INVOCATION OF THE HOLY SPIRIT (PG. 12)

Scripture   *Genesis 3: 14-15 (Douay-Rheims Version)*

And the Lord God said to the serpent: Because thou hast done this thing, thou art cursed among all cattle, and beasts of the earth: upon thy breast shalt thou go, and earth shalt thou eat all the days of thy life. I will put enmities between thee and the woman, and thy seed and her seed: she shall crush thy head, and thou shalt lie in wait for her heel.

St. Louis de Montfort   *TD: #52*

God has established only one enmity – but it is an irreconcilable one which will last and even go on increasing to the end of time. That enmity is between Mary, his worthy Mother, and the devil, between the children and the servants of the Blessed Virgin and the children and followers of Lucifer.

The most fearful enemy that God has set up against the devil is Mary, his holy Mother. From the time of the earthly paradise, although she existed then only in his mind, he gave her such a hatred for his accursed enemy, such ingenuity in exposing the wickedness of the ancient serpent and such power to defeat, overthrow and crush this proud rebel, that Satan fears her not only more than angels or men but in a certain sense more than God himself. This does not mean that the anger, hatred and power of God are not infinitely greater than the Blessed Virgin's, since her attributes are limited. It simply means that Satan, being proud, suffers infinitely more in being vanquished and punished by a lowly and humble servant of God, for her humility humiliates him more than the power of God.

Question

What do you find to be the most difficult temptation to struggle against? What is your most persistent temptation?

Resolution

In your prayer tonight, place your struggle against this temptation into the hands of the Blessed Virgin and ask her help in overcoming this inclination to sin. Continue to pray in this manner each night.

Prayer: JESUS LIVING IN MARY (PG. 13)

Night Prayer: ST. LOUIS DE MONTFORT'S ROSARY PRAYER (PG. 72)

DAY THREE
The Mother of Christ is Our Mother

Prayer: INVOCATION OF THE HOLY SPIRIT (PG. 12)

Scripture   *Romans 8: 28-30*

We know that in everything God works for good with those who love him, who are called according to his purpose. For those whom he foreknew he also predestined to be conformed to the image of his Son, in order that he might be the first-born among many brethren. And those whom he predestined he also called; and those whom he called he also justified; and those whom he justified he also glorified.

St. Louis de Montfort   *SM: #11-12*

As in the natural life a child must have a father and a mother, so in the supernatural life of grace a true child of the Church must have God for his Father and Mary for his mother. If he prides himself on having God for his Father but does not give Mary the tender affection of a true child, he is an imposter and his father is the devil.

Since Mary produced the head of the elect, Jesus Christ, she must produce the members of that head, that is, all true Christians. A mother does not conceive a head without members, nor members without a head. If anyone wishes to become a member of Jesus Christ, and consequently be filled with grace and truth, he must be formed in Mary through the grace of Jesus Christ, which she possesses with a fullness enabling her to communicate it abundantly to true members of Jesus Christ, her true children.

Question

Christ goes so far as to share even his Mother with us so that she might be our Mother as well. What does it mean for you to have Mary as your Mother?

Prayer: JESUS LIVING IN MARY (PG. 13)

Night Prayer: ST. LOUIS DE MONTFORT'S ROSARY PRAYER (PG. 72)

DAY FOUR
Mary is the Perfect Way of Christ himself

Prayer: INVOCATION OF THE HOLY SPIRIT (PG. 12)

Scripture   *Luke 2: 6-7*

And while they were there, the time came for her to be delivered. And she gave birth to her first-born son and wrapped him in swaddling cloths, and laid him in a manger, because there was no place for them in the inn.

St. Louis de Montfort   *TD: #157*

Mary is the most perfect and most holy of all creatures, and Jesus, who came to us in a perfect manner, chose no other road for his great and wonderful journey. The Most High, the Incomprehensible One, the Inaccessible One, He Who Is, deigned to come down to us poor earthly creatures who are nothing at all. How was this done?

The Most High God came down to us in a perfect way through the humble Virgin Mary, without losing any of his divinity or holiness. It is likewise through Mary that we poor creatures must ascend to Almighty God in a perfect manner without having anything to fear.

God, the Incomprehensible, allowed himself to be contained by the humble Virgin Mary without losing anything of his immensity. So we must let ourselves be perfectly contained and led by the humble Virgin without any reserve on our part.

God, the Inaccessible, drew near to us and united himself closely, perfectly and even personally to our humanity through Mary without losing anything of his majesty. So it is also through Mary that we must draw near to God and unite ourselves with him perfectly, intimately and without fear of being rejected.

Lastly, He Who Is deigned to come down to us who are not and turned our nothingness into God, or He Who Is. He did this perfectly by giving and submitting himself entirely to the young Virgin Mary, without ceasing to be in time He Who Is from all eternity. Likewise it is through Mary that we, who are nothing, may become like God by grace and glory. We accomplish this by giving ourselves to her so perfectly and so completely as to remain nothing, as far as self is concerned, and to be everything in her, without any fear of illusion.

Resolution

As St. Louis de Montfort shows us, when we confide our lives into the care of Mary we experience a profound union with Jesus Christ because we are participating in the most profound and the most basic movement of his life. In your prayer today, ask Jesus for a great confidence in and submission to the Virgin Mary.

Prayer: JESUS LIVING IN MARY (PG. 13)

Night Prayer: ST. LOUIS DE MONTFORT'S ROSARY PRAYER (PG. 72)

DAY FIVE
Mary is our Treasury

Prayer: INVOCATION OF THE HOLY SPIRIT (PG. 12)

Scripture   *Matthew 6: 19-21*

Do not lay up for yourselves treasures on earth, where moth and rust consume and where thieves break in and steal, but lay up for yourselves treasures in heaven, where neither moth nor rust consumes and where thieves do not break in and steal. For where your treasure is, there will your heart be also.

St. Louis de Montfort   *TD: #178*

Do not commit the gold of your charity, the silver of your purity to a threadbare sack or a battered old chest, or the waters of heavenly grace or the wines of your merits and virtues to a tainted and fetid cask, such as you are. Otherwise you will be robbed by thieving devils who are on the lookout day and night waiting for a favorable opportunity to plunder. If you do so, all those pure gifts from God will be spoiled by the unwholesome presence of self-love, inordinate self-reliance and self-will.

Pour into the bosom and heart of Mary all your precious possessions, all your graces and virtues. She is a spiritual vessel, a vessel of honor, a singular vessel of devotion. Ever since God himself personally hid himself with all his perfections in this vessel, it has become completely spiritual, and the abode of all spiritual souls. It has become honorable and has been the throne of honor for the greatest saints in heaven. It has become outstanding in devotion and the home of those renowned for gentleness, grace and virtue. Moreover, it has become rich as a house of gold, as strong as a tower of David and as pure as a tower of ivory.

Questions

What are your best qualities? What are the greatest blessings that you have received? What is the most prized treasure of your heart? Do you have the confidence to turn all of these over to the care and custody of Mary?

Resolution

In your prayer tonight, put all of the spiritual treasures that you receive during the day into the hands of Mary so that she can guard them and augment them for you. Continue to pray in this manner each night.

Prayer: JESUS LIVING IN MARY (PG. 13)

Night Prayer: ST. LOUIS DE MONTFORT'S ROSARY PRAYER (PG. 72)

DAY SIX
Mary communicates her spirit to us

Prayer: INVOCATION OF THE HOLY SPIRIT (PG. 12)

Scripture   *2 Peter 1: 5-8*

For this very reason make every effort to supplement your faith with virtue, and virtue with knowledge, and knowledge with self-control, and self-control with steadfastness, and steadfastness with godliness, and godliness with brotherly affection, and brotherly affection with love. For if these things are yours and abound, they keep you from being ineffective or unfruitful in the knowledge of our Lord Jesus Christ.

St. Louis de Montfort   *SM: #57*

To sum up, Mary becomes all things for the soul that wishes to serve Jesus Christ. She enlightens his mind with her pure faith. She deepens his heart with her humility. She enlarges and inflames his heart with her charity, makes it pure with her purity, makes it noble and great through her motherly care. But why dwell on this? Experience alone will teach us the wonders wrought by Mary in the soul, wonders so great that the wise and the proud and even a great number of devout people find it hard to credit them.

Question

What aspect of your spirit is most like Mary? What aspect of your spirit is most unlike, and opposed, to her?

Prayer: JESUS LIVING IN MARY (PG. 13)

Night Prayer: ST. LOUIS DE MONTFORT'S ROSARY PRAYER (PG. 72)

DAY SEVEN
Mary, the Mold of God

Prayer: INVOCATION OF THE HOLY SPIRIT (PG. 12)

Scripture   *2 Corinthians 3: 18*

And we all, with unveiled face, beholding the glory of the Lord, are being changed into his likeness from one degree of glory to another; for this comes from the Lord who is the Spirit.

St. Louis de Montfort   *TD: #219-221*

Please note that I say that the saints are molded in Mary. There is a vast difference between carving a statue by blows of hammer and chisel and making a statue by using a mold. Sculptors and statuemakers work hard and need plenty of time to make statues by the first method. But the second method does not involve much work and takes very little time. St. Augustine speaking to our Blessed Lady says, "You are worthy to be called the mold of God." Mary is a mold capable of forming people into the image of the God-man. Anyone who is cast into this divine mold is quickly shaped and molded into Jesus and Jesus into him. At little cost and in a short time he will become Christ-like since he is cast into the very same mold that fashioned a God-man.

I think I can very well compare some spiritual directors and devout persons to sculptors who wish to produce Jesus in themselves and in others by methods other than this. Many of them rely on their own skill, ingenuity and art and chip away endlessly with mallet and chisel at hard stone or badly- prepared wood, in an effort to produce a likeness of our Lord. At times, they do not manage to produce a recognizable likeness either because they lack knowledge and experience of the person of Jesus or because a clumsy stroke has spoiled the whole work. But those who accept this little-known secret of grace which I offer them can rightly be compared to smelters and molders who have discovered the beautiful mold of Mary where Jesus was so divinely and so naturally formed. They do not rely on their own skill but on the perfection of the mold. They cast and lose themselves in Mary where they become true models of her Son.

You may think this a beautiful and convincing comparison. But how many understand it? I would like you, my dear friend, to understand it. But remember that only molten and liquefied substances may be poured into a mold. That means you must crush and melt down the old Adam in you if you wish to acquire the likeness of the new Adam in Mary.

Question

Am I truly willing to experience a total transformation of my person in Christ? Does the call to such a complete personal transformation give me fear? Am I attracted by the idea of being transformed into Christ? What is stronger within me – the fear of changing or the attraction to Christ?

Prayer: Jesus Living in Mary (pg. 13)

Night Prayer: St. Louis de Montfort's Rosary Prayer (pg. 72)

• • •

These seven days faithfully observed have borne the fruit of a singular and privileged grace, a deeper and more personal knowledge of Mary. Consider for a moment how great a gift the Lord has given you in sharing his own relationship with his Mother with you. Consider how near Our Lady is to you in the concrete experiences of need, failure, blessing, struggle, joyfulness, and grace that fill your life. Turn to her now in thankful confidence, and place the fruits of these seven days in her hands:

Say 5 decades of the Rosary and the AVE MARIS STELLA *(below)*

Hail, O Star of the ocean,
God's own Mother blest,
ever sinless Virgin,
gate of heavenly rest.
Taking that sweet Ave,
which from Gabriel came,
peace confirm within us,
changing Eva's name.
Break the sinners' fetters,
make our blindness day,
Chase all evils from us,
for all blessings pray.
Show thyself a Mother,
may the Word divine
born for us thine Infant
hear our prayers through thine.
Virgin all excelling,
mildest of the mild,
free from guilt preserve us
meek and undefiled.
Keep our life all spotless,
make our way secure
till we find in Jesus,
joy for evermore.
Praise to God the Father,
honor to the Son,
in the Holy Spirit,
be the glory one.
Amen.

WEEK THREE
KNOWLEDGE OF JESUS CHRIST

...

Can we love someone we do not even know?
Can we love deeply someone we only know vaguely?

Why is Jesus,
the adorable, eternal and incarnate Wisdom,
loved so little
if not because he is either too little known
or not known at all?

KNOWLEDGE OF JESUS CHRIST

JESUS CHRIST HAS BEEN THE MOTIVATION FOR UNDERTAKING THIS process of preparation. Jesus Christ is the goal of this process. And it has been the grace of Jesus Christ that has guided and sustained us throughout these several weeks. If we have been trying to empty ourselves of the self-serving spirit of the world, it is precisely so that we may be filled with the spirit of Jesus Christ. The grace of self-knowledge for which we have been praying stems from the recognition that we can only come to know the full truth of ourselves in and through our relationship with Jesus Christ. In learning to surrender ourselves into the care of the Blessed Mother, we have been learning how to live in accordance with the spirit of Jesus Christ who is the first to surrender himself to her care.

It is here that the true power and the hidden genius of Fr. de Montfort's spirituality of consecration are opened to us. Those who can learn to identify so strongly with the Lord as to participate in his own act of radical and trust-filled surrender of himself into the care of the Blessed Mother will come to know Jesus in a remarkably intimate way. They will do so because they do not simply gaze on the life of Jesus from outside as interested and curious onlookers. Rather their participation in this fundamental movement of the Lord's own spirit allows them to experience his life from within, so to speak, as involved and invested participants. In sharing his relationship with his Mother with us, our Lord shares himself with us in a way that is immediate, direct and intimate.

This participation in the self-emptying movement of the Incarnation that we have begun in turning to Our Lady is a participation in the great and saving Mystery by which the Lord won our redemption. For the sake of our salvation, for the sake of the Cross, the Lord becomes flesh. Formed within Mary, the Lord continues the self-emptying movement begun in his Incarnation all the way to Calvary where he gives himself completely for our salvation. There can be, therefore, no true knowledge of Jesus Christ that does not involve the knowledge of his Cross. The Cross is, in the words of Fr. de Montfort, "the greatest secret of the King," the key to unlocking the mysteries of Jesus Christ. This is why the spirit of the world, which is opposed to the self-giving spirit of the Cross, cannot know Jesus Christ. Those who have begun to empty themselves in trust-filled surrender to Our Lady, however, are formed by the self-giving spirit of the Cross and, armed with this key, can begin to enter into the very heart of the life of Christ. One must be warned, however, that just as Fr. de Montfort insists that our knowledge of Jesus Christ be genuinely personal, so too he insists that our knowledge of the Cross likewise be personal and experiential.

The intimately connected Mysteries of the Incarnation and the Cross of Jesus Christ are the anchor points between which the prayerful reflection of this week will take place. However, in addition to working through the daily exercises of this week, one must also take into account the fact that the day for making the *Act of Total Consecration* is drawing near. As noted in the introduction to this book, it is important to spend a bit of time thinking about how, and where, one will do this. It is also important to make arrangements to celebrate the sacrament of Reconciliation prior to praying the *Act of Total Consecration* so that one's act of self-gift and surrender to the Lord Jesus through the hands of his Mother be an act that is made with a heart that is truly unburdened and a spirit that is truly free.

Night Prayer during these seven days is an act of ardent long-
ing for the fullness of the Lord Jesus. The beautiful and powerful
words of a prayer composed by St. Augustine, a prayer that is strongly
recommended by St. Louis de Montfort, will be the words that
express the ardent desire of our own souls for that One alone in
whom we shall find rest.

Prayer of St. Augustine

O Jesus Christ, you are my father,
my merciful God, my great king,
my good shepherd, my only master, my best helper,
my beloved friend of overwhelming beauty,
my living bread, my eternal priest.

You are my guide to my heavenly home,
my one true light, my holy joy, my true way,
my shining wisdom, my unfeigned simplicity,
the peace and harmony of my soul,
my perfect safeguard, my bounteous inheritance,
my everlasting salvation.

My loving Lord, Jesus Christ,
why have I ever loved or desired
anything else in my life but you, my God?
Where was I when I was not in communion with you?

From now on, I direct all my desires
to be inspired by you and centered on you.
I direct them to press forward
for they have tarried long enough,
to hasten towards their goal,
to seek the one they yearn for.

O Jesus,
let him who does not love you be accursed,
and filled with bitterness.

O gentle Jesus,
let every worthy feeling of mine
show you love, take delight in you and admire you.

O God of my heart and my inheritance, Christ Jesus,
may my heart mellow before the influence of your spirit
and may you live in me.
May the flame of your love burn in my soul.
May it burn incessantly on the altar of my heart.
May it glow in my innermost being.
May it spread its heat into the hidden recesses of my soul
and on the day of my consummation
may I appear before you consumed in your love.
Amen.

We have not spent the last week asking the Lord for the grace of a deeply personal relationship with the Blessed Mother only to set our relationship with Mary aside as we move into this week focused on coming to know more fully her Son. Rather, we recognize that the presence of Mary in our lives opens our eyes to more fully perceive the presence of Our Lord. Therefore, at the beginning of this week, and before moving to the first day's spiritual exercises, we turn once more to Our Lady so that the glory of her Son might shine forth in our lives, and we will do this by praying the *Litany of the Blessed Virgin.* While one is certainly free to make the Litany part of his daily prayer over these seven days, it is only necessary to pray it on the first.

Upon completing the exercises for the seventh day, one places the fruits of this time in the hands of the Blessed Virgin by praying the *Ave Maris Stella.*

At the very beginning of the preparation process, in preparation to struggle against the spirit of the world, a prayerful pause was made to invoke the grace of God upon this effort. Once the process of preparation has come to its conclusion it is important to pause once more and to prayerfully consider what has taken place in one's spiritual life over these thirty-three days. Having done so, we turn once more to the Lord who saves us, invoking his blessing and protection as well as his grace that our *Act of Total Consecration* be a true and unreserved gift of ourselves. We will do this by praying the *Litany of the Sacred Heart.* This great litany, which Fr. de Montfort himself recommends be part of the process of preparation, celebrates the wondrous totality with which Our Lord, out of love, gives himself completely to us for our salvation. If one has allowed the space of a few days between the conclusion of the preparation process and the date of his *Act of Total Consecration* – for example, to be assured of the opportunity to confess or to reflect for a day or two upon the fruits of this process – this Litany should be prayed slowly and devoutly each day.

LITANY OF THE BLESSED VIRGIN

It is recommended to pray this Litany before an image of Our Lady.

Lord, have mercy	Lord, have mercy
Christ, have mercy	Christ, have mercy
Lord, have mercy	Lord, have mercy
God our Father in heaven	have mercy on us
God the Son, Redeemer of the world	have mercy on us
God the Holy Spirit	have mercy on us
Holy Trinity, one God	have mercy on us
Holy Mary	pray for us
Holy Mother of God	pray for us
Most honored of virgins	pray for us
Chosen daughter of the Father	pray for us
Mother of Christ the King	pray for us
Glory of the Holy Spirit	pray for us
Virgin daughter of Zion	pray for us
Virgin poor and humble	pray for us
Virgin gentle and obedient	pray for us
Handmaid of the Lord	pray for us
Mother of the Lord	pray for us
Helper of the Redeemer	pray for us
Full of grace	pray for us
Fountain of beauty	pray for us
Model of virtue	pray for us

Finest fruit of the redemption	pray for us
Perfect disciple of Christ	pray for us
Untarnished image of the Church	pray for us
Woman transformed	pray for us
Woman clothed with the sun	pray for us
Woman crowned with stars	pray for us
Gentle Lady	pray for us
Gracious Lady	pray for us
Our Lady	pray for us
Joy of Israel	pray for us
Splendor of the Church	pray for us
Pride of the human race	pray for us
Advocate of peace	pray for us
Minister of holiness	pray for us
Champion of God's people	pray for us
Queen of love	pray for us
Queen of mercy	pray for us
Queen of peace	pray for us
Queen of angels	pray for us
Queen of patriarchs and prophets	pray for us
Queen of apostles and martyrs	pray for us
Queen of confessors and virgins	pray for us
Queen of all saints	pray for us
Queen conceived without original sin	pray for us
Queen assumed into heaven	pray for us

Queen of all the earth	pray for us
Queen of heaven	pray for us
Queen of the universe	pray for us

Lamb of God,
  you take away the sins of the world   spare us, O Lord
Lamb of God,
  you take away the sins of the world   hear us, O Lord
Lamb of God,
  you take away the sins of the world   have mercy on us

Pray for us, O glorious Mother of the Lord.
That we may become worthy of the promises of Christ.

God of mercy,
listen to the prayers of your servants
who have honored your handmaid Mary
as mother and queen.
Grant that by your grace
we may serve you and our neighbor on earth
and be welcomed into your eternal kingdom.
We ask this through Christ our Lord.
Amen.

DAY ONE
Jesus Christ – The Beginning and the end

Prayer: INVOCATION OF THE HOLY SPIRIT (PG. 12)

Scripture   *John 15: 1-5*

I am the true vine, and my Father is the vinedresser. Every branch of mine that bears no fruit, he takes away, and every branch that does bear fruit he prunes, that it may bear more fruit. You are already made clean by the word which I have spoken to you. Abide in me, and I in you. As the branch cannot bear fruit by itself, unless it abides in the vine, neither can you, unless you abide in me. I am the vine, you are the branches. He who abides in me, and I in him, he it is that bears much fruit, for apart from me you can do nothing.

St. Louis de Montfort   *TD: #61*

Jesus, our Savior, true God and true man must be the ultimate end of all our other devotions; otherwise they would be false and misleading. He is the Alpha and the Omega, the beginning and the end of everything...

For in him alone dwells the entire fullness of the divinity and the complete fullness of grace, virtue and perfection. In him alone we have been blessed with every spiritual blessing; he is the only teacher from whom we must learn; the only Lord on whom we should depend; the only Head to whom we should be united and the only model that we should imitate. He is the only Physician that can heal us; the only Shepherd that can feed us; the only Way that can lead us; the only Truth that we can believe; the only Life that can animate us. He alone is everything to us and he alone can satisfy all our desires.

We are given no other name under heaven by which we can be saved. God has laid no other foundation for our salvation, perfection and glory than Jesus. Every edifice which is not built on that firm rock is founded on shifting sands and will certainly fall sooner or later. Every one of the faithful who is not united to him is like a branch broken from the stem of the vine. It falls and withers and is fit only to be burnt. If we live in Jesus and Jesus lives in us, we need not fear damnation. Neither angels in heaven nor men on earth, nor devils in hell, no creature whatever can harm us, for no creature can separate us from the love of God which is in Christ Jesus. Through him, with him and in him, we can do all things and render all honor and glory to the Father in the unity of the Holy Spirit; we can make ourselves perfect and be for our neighbor a fragrance of eternal life.

Questions

In the decisions that you make every day, do you unite yourself with Jesus? In your daily activities and your work, do you remain united with Christ? What separates you from Jesus?

Prayer: Jᴇsᴜs Lɪᴠɪɴɢ ɪɴ Mᴀʀʏ (ᴘɢ. 13)

Night Prayer: Pʀᴀʏᴇʀ ᴏғ Sᴛ. Aᴜɢᴜsᴛɪɴᴇ (ᴘɢ. 94)

DAY TWO
The Greatness of the Incarnation

Prayer: INVOCATION OF THE HOLY SPIRIT (PG. 12)

Scripture   *1 John 1: 1-4*

That which was from the beginning, which we have heard, which we have seen with our eyes, which we have looked upon and touched with our hands, concerning the word of life — the life was made manifest, and we saw it, and testify to it, and proclaim to you the eternal life which was with the Father and was made manifest to us — that which we have seen and heard we proclaim also to you, so that you may have fellowship with us; and our fellowship is with the Father and with his Son Jesus Christ. And we are writing this that our joy may be complete.

St. Louis de Montfort   *TD: #248*

Time does not permit me to linger here and elaborate on the perfections and wonders of the mystery of Jesus living and reigning in Mary, or the Incarnation of the Word. I shall confine myself to the following brief remarks. The Incarnation is the first mystery of Jesus Christ; it is the most hidden; and it is the most exalted and the least known.

It was in this mystery that Jesus, in the womb of Mary and with her cooperation, chose all the elect. For this reason the saints call her womb the throne-room of God's mysteries.

It was in this mystery that Jesus anticipated all subsequent mysteries of his life by his willing acceptance of them. Consequently, this mystery is a summary of all his mysteries since it contains the intention and the grace of them all.

Lastly, this mystery is the seat of the mercy, the liberality and the glory of God. It is the seat of his mercy for us, since we can approach and speak to Jesus through Mary. We need her intervention to see or speak to him. Here, ever responsive to the prayer of his Mother, Jesus unfailingly grants grace and mercy to all poor sinners. "Let us come boldly before the throne of grace."

It is the seat of liberality for Mary, because while the new Adam dwelt in this truly earthly paradise God performed there so many hidden marvels beyond the understanding of men and angels. For this reason, the saints call Mary "the magnificence of God", as if God showed his magnificence only in Mary.

It is the seat of glory to his Father, because it was in Mary that Jesus perfectly atoned to his Father on behalf of mankind. It was here that he perfectly restored the glory that sin had taken from his Father. It was here that our Lord, by the sacrifice of himself and of his will, gave more glory to God than he would have given had he offered all the sacrifices of the Old Law. Finally in Mary he gave his Father infinite glory such as his Father had never received from man.

Resolution

I will be more conscious throughout today of the presence of Christ in all aspects of my life.

Prayer: Jᴇsus Lɪvɪɴɢ ɪɴ Mᴀʀʏ (ᴘɢ. 13)

Night Prayer: Pʀᴀʏᴇʀ ᴏꜰ Sᴛ. Aᴜɢᴜsᴛɪɴᴇ (ᴘɢ. 94)

DAY THREE
The profound obedience of Christ

Prayer: INVOCATION OF THE HOLY SPIRIT (PG. 12)

Scripture   *Luke 2: 51-52*

And he went down with them and came to Nazareth, and was obedient to them; and his mother kept all these things in her heart. And Jesus increased in wisdom and in stature, and in favor with God and man.

St. Louis de Montfort   *TD: #139*

Our good Master stooped to enclose himself in the womb of the Blessed Virgin, a captive but loving slave, and to make himself subject to her for thirty years. The human mind is bewildered when it reflects seriously upon this conduct of Incarnate Wisdom. He did not choose to give himself in a direct manner to the human race though he could easily have done so. He chose to come through the Virgin Mary. Thus he did not come into the world independently of others in the flower of his manhood, but he came as a frail little child dependent on the care and attention of his Mother. Consumed with the desire to give glory to God, his Father, and save the human race, he saw no better or shorter way to do so than by submitting completely to Mary.

He did this not just for the first eight, ten or fifteen years of his life like other children, but for thirty years. He gave more glory to God, his Father, during all those years of submission and dependence than he would have given by spending them working miracles, preaching far and wide, and converting all mankind. Otherwise he would have done these things.

What immeasurable glory then do we give to God when, following the example of Jesus, we submit to Mary! With such a convincing and well-known example before us, can we be so foolish as to believe there is a better and shorter way of giving God glory than by submitting ourselves to Mary as Jesus did?

Questions

Are you an obedient person? Or rebellious? Are you a person who is faithful? Or unfaithful? Can you submit yourself to Mary like Jesus and with Jesus? Can you surrender your own will, like Jesus, to comply with the will of God?

Prayer: JESUS LIVING IN MARY (PG. 13)

Night Prayer: PRAYER OF ST. AUGUSTINE (PG. 94)

DAY FOUR
The love of Christ for the Cross

Prayer: INVOCATION OF THE HOLY SPIRIT (PG. 12)

Scripture   *Mark 8: 31-33*

And he began to teach them that the Son of man must suffer many things, and be rejected by the elders and the chief priests and the scribes, and be killed, and after three days rise again. And he said this plainly. And Peter took him, and began to rebuke him. But turning and seeing his disciples, he rebuked Peter, and said, "Get behind me, Satan! For you are not on the side of God, but of men."

St. Louis de Montfort   *LEW: #169*

Incarnate Wisdom loved the Cross from his infancy. At his coming into the world, while in his Mother's womb, he received it from his eternal Father. He placed it deep in his heart, there to dominate his life, saying, "My God and my Father, I chose this Cross when I was in your bosom. I choose it now in the womb of my Mother. I love it with all my strength and I place it deep in my heart to be my spouse and my mistress."

Resolution

In your prayer today, ask the Lord, through the intercession of Mary, for the grace of a genuine love for the Cross.

Prayer: JESUS LIVING IN MARY (PG. 13)

Night Prayer: PRAYER OF ST. AUGUSTINE (PG. 94)

DAY FIVE
Christ loves us to the Extreme

Prayer: INVOCATION OF THE HOLY SPIRIT (PG. 12)

Scripture   *Isaiah 53: 3-12*

He was despised and rejected by men; a man of sorrows, and acquainted with grief; and as one from whom men hide their faces he was despised, and we esteemed him not. Surely he has borne our griefs and carried our sorrows; yet we esteemed him stricken, smitten by God, and afflicted. But he was wounded for our transgressions, he was bruised for our iniquities; upon him was the chastisement that made us whole, and with his stripes we are healed. All we like sheep have gone astray; we have turned every one to his own way; and the Lord has laid on him the iniquity of us all. He was oppressed, and he was afflicted, yet he opened not his mouth; like a lamb that is led to the slaughter, and like a sheep that before its shearers is dumb, so he opened not his mouth. By oppression and judgment he was taken away; and as for his generation, who considered that he was cut off out of the land of the living, stricken for the transgression of my people? And they made his grave with the wicked and with a rich man in his death, although he had done no violence, and there was no deceit in his mouth. Yet it was the will of the Lord to bruise him; he has put him to grief; when he makes himself an offering for sin, he shall see his offspring, he shall prolong his days; the will of the Lord shall prosper in his hand; he shall see the fruit of the travail of his soul and be satisfied; by his knowledge shall the righteous one, my servant, make many to be accounted righteous; and he shall bear their iniquities. Therefore I will divide him a portion with the great, and he shall divide the spoil with the strong; because he poured out his soul to death, and was numbered with the transgressors; yet he bore the sin of many, and made intercession for the transgressors.

St. Louis de Montfort *FC: #57*

Reflect on the wounds and sufferings of Christ crucified. He himself has told us, *All you who pass by the way* of thorns and the cross, *look and see.* Look with the eyes of your body, and see through the eyes of your contemplation whether your poverty, destitution, disgrace, sorrow, desolation are like mine; look upon me who am innocent, and lament, you who are guilty!

The Holy Spirit tells us, through the Apostles, to contemplate the crucified Christ. He bids us arm ourselves with this thought, for it is the most powerful and formidable weapon against our enemies. When you are assailed by poverty, disrepute, sorrow, temptation, and other crosses, arm yourselves with the shield, breastplate, helmet and two-edged sword, which is the remembrance of Christ crucified. It is there you will find the solution of every problem and the means to conquer all your enemies.

Resolution

Dedicate time today to making a thorough examination of conscience and to recognizing that your sins cause the suffering of Christ. Ask the Lord for a genuine horror of sin and its consequences. Go to confession before making the *Act of Total Consecration.*

Prayer: JESUS LIVING IN MARY (PG. 13)

Night Prayer: PRAYER OF ST. AUGUSTINE (PG. 94)

DAY SIX
The Blessed Sacrament

Prayer: INVOCATION OF THE HOLY SPIRIT (PG. 12)

Scripture   *1 Corinthians 11: 23-26*

For I received from the Lord what I also delivered to you, that the Lord Jesus on the night when he was betrayed took bread, and when he had given thanks, he broke it, and said, "This is my body which is for you. Do this in remembrance of me." In the same way also the cup, after supper, saying, "This cup is the new covenant in my blood. Do this, as often as you drink it, in remembrance of me." For as often as you eat this bread and drink the cup, you proclaim the Lord's death until he comes.

St. Louis de Montfort   *LEW: #71*

Eternal Wisdom, on the one hand, wished to prove his love for man by dying in his place in order to save him, but on the other hand, he could not bear the thought of leaving him. So he devised a marvelous way of dying and living at the same time, and of abiding with man until the end of time. So, in order to fully satisfy his love, he instituted the sacrament of Holy Eucharist and went to the extent of changing and overturning nature itself.

He does not conceal himself under a sparkling diamond or some other precious stone, because he does not want to abide with man in an ostentatious manner. But he hides himself under the appearance of a small piece of bread – man's ordinary nourishment – so that when received he might enter the heart of man and there take his delight. *Ardenter amantium hoc est* - Those who love ardently act in this way. "O eternal Wisdom," says a saint, "O God who is truly lavish with himself in his desire to be with man."

Questions

With what disposition and degree of attentiveness do you typically receive your Lord in Holy Communion? How frequently do you attend Mass and receive communion? How much time do you spend praying before the Blessed Sacrament?

Resolution

Determine how you can receive Holy Communion with greater attention and devotion, and do so. If you are unable to receive Communion, determine what you are going to do to change this situation. And do it.

Prayer: JESUS LIVING IN MARY (PG. 13)

Night Prayer: PRAYER OF ST. AUGUSTINE (PG. 94)

DAY SEVEN
Participate in the Life of Christ

Prayer: INVOCATION OF THE HOLY SPIRIT (PG. 12)

Scripture   *Philippians 2: 5-11*

Have this mind among yourselves, which was in Christ Jesus, who, though he was in the form of God, did not count equality with God a thing to be grasped, but emptied himself, taking the form of a servant, being born in the likeness of men. And being found in human form he humbled himself and became obedient unto death, even death on a cross. Therefore God has highly exalted him and bestowed on him the name which is above every name, that at the name of Jesus every knee should bow, in heaven and on earth and under the earth, and every tongue confess that Jesus Christ is Lord, to the glory of God the Father.

St. Louis de Montfort   *SR: #65*

The chief concern of the Christian should be to tend to perfection. Be faithful imitators of God as his well beloved children, the great Apostle tells us.... Saint Gregory of Nyssa makes a delightful comparison when he says that we are all artists and that our souls are blank canvasses which we have to fill in. The colors which we use are the Christian virtues and the original which we have to copy is Jesus Christ, the perfect living image of God the Father. Just as a painter who wants to do a life-like portrait places the model before his eyes and looks at it before making each stroke, so the Christian must always have before his eyes the life and virtues of Jesus Christ, so as never to say, think or do anything which is not in conformity with his model.

111

Questions

Having come this far, how do you feel? Are you ready to surrender yourself completely to Christ through the hands of Mary?

Resolution

Tomorrow, or during the next few days, make the *Act of Total Consecration* and honor the Blessed Virgin by means of a sacrifice, an almsgiving, or of the saying of an extra rosary. Make a firm decision to remain faithful to the obligation of growing in this spirituality of consecration.

Prayer: JESUS LIVING IN MARY (PG. 13)

Night Prayer: PRAYER OF ST. AUGUSTINE (PG. 94)
AVE MARIS STELLA (PG. 113)

AVE MARIS STELLA

Hail, O Star of the ocean,
God's own Mother blest,
ever sinless Virgin,
gate of heavenly rest.
Taking that sweet Ave,
which from Gabriel came,
peace confirm within us,
changing Eva's name.
Break the sinners' fetters,
make our blindness day,
Chase all evils from us,
for all blessings pray.
Show thyself a Mother,
may the Word divine
born for us thine Infant
hear our prayers through thine.
Virgin all excelling,
mildest of the mild,
free from guilt preserve us
meek and undefiled.
Keep our life all spotless,
make our way secure
till we find in Jesus,
joy for evermore.
Praise to God the Father,
honor to the Son,
in the Holy Spirit,
be the glory one.
Amen.

LITANY OF THE SACRED HEART

It is best, if at all possible, to pray this Litany in church at an altar dedicated to the Sacred Heart of Jesus and in the presence of the Blessed Sacrament. Otherwise, the Litany should be prayed before an image of the Sacred Heart, or while holding a Crucifix.

Lord, have mercy	Lord, have mercy
Christ, have mercy	Christ, have mercy
Lord, have mercy	Lord, have mercy
God our Father in heaven,	have mercy on us
God the Son, Redeemer of the world	have mercy on us
God the Holy Spirit	have mercy on us
Holy Trinity, One God	have mercy on us
Heart of Jesus, Son of the eternal Father	have mercy on us
Heart of Jesus, formed by the Holy Spirit in the womb of the Virgin Mother	have mercy on us
Heart of Jesus, one with the eternal Word	have mercy on us
Heart of Jesus, infinite in majesty	have mercy on us
Heart of Jesus, holy temple of God	have mercy on us
Heart of Jesus, tabernacle of the Most High	have mercy on us
Heart of Jesus, house of God and gate of heaven	have mercy on us
Heart of Jesus, aflame with love for us	have mercy on us
Heart of Jesus, source of justice and love	have mercy on us
Heart of Jesus, full of goodness and love	have mercy on us
Heart of Jesus, wellspring of all virtue	have mercy on us
Heart of Jesus, worthy of all praise	have mercy on us
Heart of Jesus, king and center of all hearts	have mercy on us

Heart of Jesus, treasurehouse of wisdom
   and knowledge   have mercy on us
Heart of Jesus, in whom there dwells
   the fullness of God   have mercy on us
Heart of Jesus, in whom the Father
   is well pleased   have mercy on us
Heart of Jesus, from whose fullness
   we have all received   have mercy on us
Heart of Jesus, desire of the eternal hills   have mercy on us
Heart of Jesus, patient and full of mercy   have mercy on us
Heart of Jesus, generous to all who
   turn to you   have mercy on us
Heart of Jesus, fountain of life and holiness   have mercy on us

Heart of Jesus, atonement for our sins   have mercy on us
Heart of Jesus, overwhelmed with insults   have mercy on us
Heart of Jesus, broken for our sins   have mercy on us
Heart of Jesus, obedient even to death   have mercy on us
Heart of Jesus, pierced by a lance   have mercy on us
Heart of Jesus, source of all consolation   have mercy on us

Heart of Jesus, our life and resurrection   have mercy on us
Heart of Jesus, our peace and reconciliation   have mercy on us
Heart of Jesus, victim of our sins   have mercy on us
Heart of Jesus, salvation of all who
   trust in you   have mercy on us
Heart of Jesus, hope of all who die in you   have mercy on us
Heart of Jesus, delight of all the saints   have mercy on us

Lamb of God,
   you take away the sins of the world   have mercy on us
Lamb of God,

you take away the sins of the world   have mercy on us
Lamb of God,
    you take away the sins of the world   have mercy on us

Jesus, gentle and humble of heart
Touch our hearts and make them like your own.

Father,
we rejoice in the gifts of love
we have received from the heart of Jesus your Son.
Open our hearts to share his life
and continue to bless us with his love.
We ask this in the name of Jesus the Lord.
Amen.

MAY GOD,
WHO HAS BEGUN THIS GOOD WORK IN YOU
bring it to completion through Christ Jesus our Lord!

You have arrived at the end
of the process of preparation
and stand ready to make the
Act of Total Consecration to Jesus Christ through Mary.

The day in which one makes this
Act of Total Consecration
for the first time
is truly a day of grace,
a singular and profound step in one's spiritual life.

But this step is not a final step,
but, rather, a first step,
a step that carries us more deeply into
the life and the mission of Jesus Christ,
a step that makes us children
and servants of Mary most holy.

Because of this step
we will never walk alone
because Mary walks always with us,
and more, we walk together
with all of those others who are her children and servants

following in the very footsteps of Jesus himself,
guided and inspired by his Holy Spirit
for the greater glory of the Eternal Father.

By means of this step
we belong completely to Jesus Christ
and all that we have is his
through Mary his most holy Mother.
Would that you walk always, and in fidelity,
along this way that is so sure and so perfect.

ARE YOU READY TO MAKE
The Act of Total Consecration?

Have you gone to Confession?

Have you set aside enough time
so that your prayer will not be rushed?

Will you be making the *Act of Total Consecration* by yourself?
Or with your family? Or with a group from church?
If you are making it with others,
will you take some time for private prayer beforehand?

Where will you make your *Act of Total Consecration?*
If it is at home, how will you prepare the space?
If it is in a church, will you make it before the tabernacle?
Or before an image of Our Lady?
Or before the Crucifix?

What will you do as a gesture of honor and gratitude to Our Lady?

What will you do after making *the Act of Total Consecration?*

Will you celebrate in any particular way?

Will you spend some time in quiet thanksgiving?

THE ACT OF
TOTAL CONSECRATION
OF ONESELF
To Jesus Christ through Mary

Detail of St. Louis de Montfort from the Queen of All Hearts statue at
Sanctuaire Marie Reine de Couers, Montreal Canada.

THE ACT OF
TOTAL CONSECRATION
OF ONESELF
To Jesus Christ through Mary

O Wisdom, eternal and incarnate!
O most beloved and adorable Jesus, true God and true man,
only Son of the eternal Father and of Mary ever virgin!

I adore you profoundly in the bosom and splendors
of your Father during eternity
and in the virginal womb of Mary, your most worthy Mother,
at the time of your incarnation.

I give you thanks
that you have emptied yourself in taking the form of a slave,
in order to rescue me from the cruel slavery of the devil.

I praise you and glorify you
that you have been pleased to submit yourself, in all things,
to Mary, your most holy Mother,
in order to make me, through her, your faithful slave.

But alas! Ungrateful and faithless that I am,
I have not kept the vows and the promises
that I made so solemnly to you in my baptism.

I have not fulfilled my obligations;
I do not deserve to be called your child or even your slave;
and, as there is nothing in me that does not merit
your rejection and your anger,
I no longer dare to approach your holy and august Majesty
by myself.

This is why I have recourse to the intercession and mercy
of your most holy Mother,
whom you have given to me as Mediatrix before you;
and it is through her that I hope to obtain from you
contrition and the pardon of my sins,
and the acquisition and preservation of wisdom.

I call to you, O Mary Immaculate,
living tabernacle of the Divinity,
where eternal Wisdom is hidden
and wishes to be adored by angels and by men.

I call to you, O Queen of heaven and earth,
to whose rule everything is subject that is under God.

I call to you, O sure Refuge of sinners, whose mercy fails no one;
fulfill the desires that I have for divine Wisdom,
and for that end, receive the vows and the offerings
which my lowliness presents to you.

I_____, unfaithful sinner,

renew and ratify today, in your hands,
the vows of my baptism.
I renounce forever Satan, his pomps and his works,

and I give myself entirely to Jesus Christ, incarnate Wisdom,
to carry my cross after him all the days of my life,
and to be more faithful to him than I have been until now.

I choose you today,
in the presence of the entire heavenly court,
to be my Mother and my Mistress.
I hand over to you and consecrate, as your slave,
my body and my soul,
my goods, both interior and exterior,
and even the value of my good actions, past, present and future,
leaving to you an entire and full right to dispose of me
and of everything that belongs to me, without exception,
according to your good pleasure,
for the greater glory of God, in time and in eternity.
Receive, O benign Virgin,
this little offering of my slavery,
in honor of, and in union with, the submission
that eternal Wisdom deigned to have to your maternity;
in homage to the power that the two of you
have over this little worm and wretched sinner,
and in thanksgiving for the privileges which
the Blessed Trinity has favored upon you.

I declare that I wish henceforth, as your true slave,
to seek your Honor and to obey you in all things.

O admirable Mother!
present me to your dear Son, as his eternal slave,
so that, having redeemed me through you,
he may receive me through you.

O Mother of mercy!
grant me the grace of obtaining the true wisdom of God
and so include me in the number of those whom you love,
whom you instruct, whom you lead, whom you nourish
and protect as your children and your slaves.

O Virgin most faithful!
Make me in all things so perfect
a disciple, imitator and slave of
incarnate Wisdom, Jesus Christ, your Son,
that I may come, through your intercession and your example,
to the fullness of his age on earth
and of his glory in heaven.
Amen.

QUI POTEST CAPERE CAPIAT
(He who is able to receive this, let him receive it.)

QUIS SAPIENS ET INTELLIGET HAEC?
(Who is wise that he shall understand these things?)

_____
Signature

_____
Place

_____
Date

LIVING THE TOTAL CONSECRATION

---

*Experience will teach you
infinitely more than I can tell you,
and you will find, if you have been faithful
to the little that I have told you,
so many riches and graces in this practice
that you will be surprised and
your soul will be overflowing with joy.*

RENEWAL

IN HIS MASTERWORK, *TRUE DEVOTION TO THE BLESSED VIRGIN MARY*, Fr. de Montfort no sooner finishes speaking about making an *Act of Total Consecration* than he immediately begins speaking about its renewal. For St. Louis de Montfort, consecration is never simply the gesture of a moment, but a fundamental movement of self-giving and self-surrender, an act of radical belonging to the Lord through Our Lady, that asserts itself in every aspect of life. Every gesture, every thought, every decision, every concrete action, however great or small it may be, is given into the hands of Mary for the glory of Almighty God. All of this has been surrendered to Our Lady in the *Act of Total Consecration* and this act of surrender frees us from the need to be overly preoccupied with fretting over whether or not we have offered into her care any particular word or gesture. In a marriage, or likewise in the case of religious profession of vows, however, the oath of self-gift that is pronounced with solemnity in the Church lacks its real power and meaning if it does not produce a habit of self-gift that finds renewal and grows stronger in the flesh and blood of everyday living. Similarly, the *Act of Total Consecration* must be deepened and renewed through a daily pattern of attentiveness to our complete belonging to Our Lady. This attentiveness is produced and sustained through the daily renewal of one's consecration.

Each day, Fr. de Montfort recommends, one should renew his consecration in a manner that is simple, attentive and genuine. No lengthy prayer need be recited to do this as the following, or similar, words are sufficient:

> I am all yours, and all that I have is yours, O my dear Jesus, through Mary, your holy Mother.
> (or in Latin: *Tuus totus ego sum, et omnia mea tua sunt.*)

St. Louis de Montfort also recommends that one pay particular attention to the moment of mutual self gift which is the very heart of the act of receiving Holy Communion. As often as one receives the Lord in Holy Communion, Fr. de Montfort recommends, one should take the opportunity to renew his consecration, perhaps even making it a point to join the devout praying of Our Lady's *Magnificat* to this act of renewal. These acts of renewal should be united to a more solemn renewal of one's *Act of Total Consecration* on the occasion of its anniversary each year. This renewal should be preceded and prepared for by a revisiting of the key elements of this process of preparation, either as a full thirty-three day series of spiritual exercises or in a more abbreviated form.

A particularly beautiful way of renewing one's consecration on a regular, even daily, basis is through the devout recitation of a prayer known as the *Little Crown of the Blessed Virgin Mary*. Fr. de Montfort esteemed this prayer so highly that he recommends that it be said daily, if at all possible, by those who have made the *Act of Total Consecration*. This prayer pays great honor to Our Lady in its simple structure of being composed around twelve Hail Marys which recall the twelve stars of her crown of heavenly glory. United to these Hail Marys are antiphons that celebrate her privileges and her effective intercession on our behalf. It concludes with an invocation of Our Lady that quite readily serves as a renewal of one's *Act of Total Consecration*. The text of the *Little Crown of the Blessed Virgin Mary* is given in the Appendix of this book.

Another prayer, which is also given in the Appendix, that one should make use of frequently in the living and renewing of his consecration is *Fr. de Montfort's Prayer to the Blessed Virgin*. This prayer is a cry from the saint's own heart to Our Lady and contains within it the essential core of his spirituality of consecration. It is also the prayer of one who, while he has already consecrated himself to Our Lady, recognizes that he still does not belong to her as completely as he should. As such it provides a powerful means of articulating one's own desire to renew and deepen his commitment to the faithful living out of this way of radical surrender to Almighty God, while at the same time asking for those graces that are most necessary in doing so.

A particularly powerful and effective way to renew one's consecration is through the praying of the Holy Rosary. This is especially true for those who have already incorporated the praying of the rosary into their regular spiritual exercises. For Fr. de Montfort the mysteries of Jesus, when one meditates on them in the presence of Our Lady, have a transformative power about them that roots within us the virtues of Jesus himself. The Rosary is truly a prayer of Jesus living in Mary, a prayer that is prayed within the presence of Mary and through which the Holy Spirit transforms us into the likeness of Jesus whom we meet in the communion of his mysteries. St. Louis de Montfort composed a prayer of his own to be said at the conclusion of one's meditation upon the mysteries of the Holy Rosary. This prayer is already familiar to us as we have already prayed it as our night prayer of the week devoted to knowledge of Our Lady. When prayed at the conclusion of Fr. de Montfort's method of saying the Rosary (which is included in the Appendix) it provides a singularly effective way of combining the renewal of one's *Act of Total Consecration* with the devout meditation, in the company of Our Lady, upon the riches of the Gospel in a way that enhances both.

Devotion to the Mystery of the Incarnation

THE PATH OF TOTAL CONSECRATION DRAWS ITS STRENGTH FROM an intimate participation in the life of Jesus Christ himself, who, in the Mystery of his Incarnation, took upon himself the form of a slave and entrusted himself completely into the hands of his Blessed Mother. The act of self-gift and self-surrender that one makes in the *Act of Total Consecration* is an act made in union with and in honor of this great act of self-gift and self-surrender of Jesus Christ who consecrates himself, in Mary, to the glorification of his Father and to the achievement of our salvation. The Mystery of Jesus alive in Mary, the redemptive Incarnation, is the vital beating heart of St. Louis de Montfort's spirituality of consecration. The life of the one who is consecrated must be, therefore, a life lived in celebration of this great Mystery. Regardless of the particular date on which one may make his *Act of Total Consecration*, the common feast day of all the consecrated is March 25, the Feast of the Annunciation on which the Church celebrates the Mystery of the Lord becoming flesh for our salvation. This is a feast day that must be observed, Fr. de Montfort insists, with particular fervor. This a most appropriate occasion on which to make a formal renewal of one's *Act of Total Consecration*.

The celebration of the redemptive Incarnation of the Lord, however, should be a daily matter for the consecrated. Two very simple ways of doing this are by developing a great love of the praying of a single Hail Mary at various times throughout the day and by cultivating the habit of the regular practice of acts of self-denial. Mortification, the act of denying ourselves, is more than a useful spiritual discipline; it is a concrete way of uniting ourselves with the Lord who laid aside his glory and *emptied himself* in his Incarnation. It enfleshes, so to speak, within us something of the great humility of Jesus who took upon himself *the form of a slave* in Mary's womb (Phil 2: 7), making himself poor so that we might become rich (2 Cor 8:

9). In praying the inspired words of the Hail Mary, Fr. de Montfort teaches, we stand with Gabriel and Mary at the point of the Eternal Word becoming flesh. In praying these inspired words we call out with St. Elizabeth in wonder and joy at the mystery of Jesus living in Mary and feel the touch of his grace reach out to heal and renew us.

The Association of Mary, Queen of All Hearts

THOSE WHO MAKE THE ACT OF TOTAL CONSECRATION ARE ENcouraged to enroll as members of the Association of Mary, Queen of All Hearts. The association is a spiritual fellowship that gathers together all of those who, having made their consecration, commit themselves to the practice of true devotion to the Blessed Virgin Mary as taught by St. Louis de Montfort. It shares the mission of the Company of Mary, the religious community of missionaries founded by St. Louis de Montfort, of working to bring about the reign of Jesus through Mary. Spiritually united to the priests and brothers of the Company of Mary, members of the Association of Mary, Queen of All Hearts, unite their prayers and good works and their faithful living of the consecration under the grace-filled mantle of Our Lady's guidance and protection so that her Queenship may become a more manifest reality in our world. Its members also receive the benefit of a sharing in the good works and prayers of the members of the Company of Mary as they exercise their commission to bring the richness of the Montfortian tradition to the Church wherever it is found. Membership in the association is an excellent way to remain conscious of the fundamental unity that all of those who have made the *Act of Total Consecration* share by means of their common belonging to Jesus in Mary, and to remind ourselves that even our private acts of devotion are fundamentally united to and enriched by the activity of the entire Body of Christ. An enrollment card for the Association of Mary, Queen of All Hearts is included at the end of this book.

An External sign of one's Consecration

A PRACTICE WHICH, WHILE HE NAMED IT NOT NECESSARY, WAS greatly esteemed by St. Louis de Montfort is the wearing of what he termed "a little chain" as an outward sign of one's having accepted "the glorious slavery of Jesus Christ." This wearing of a chain, for Fr. de Montfort, acted as a constant reminder of our being unbreakably bound to Jesus Christ, a sign that we are not ashamed to be recognized as servants of Jesus and Mary and an act of recognition that we have been set free from the cruel chains of our slavery to sin and Satan. There is much to recommend the wearing of a sign of one's consecration – be it, for example, a simple chain worn around one's wrist or a cross or a medal of Our Lady worn outwardly and attached to a chain. Such a sign, however, must not be ostentatious and it should be made of simple, sturdy materials. A chain worn as the outward sign of one's consecration is not mere jewelry and, in its simplicity is, in the words of Fr. de Montfort, "far more glorious than all the gold ornaments worn by monarchs."

All things *through*, *with*, *in*, and *for* Mary

ALL OF THE WAYS OF LIVING ONE'S CONSECRATION OUTLINED above are ultimately at the service of the cultivation of several very important virtues, or habits of the heart, that contain the very essence of the life of consecration to which St. Louis de Montfort calls us. With a direct simplicity, the great saint describes these virtues as doing all things *through* Mary, *with* Mary, *in* Mary, and *for* Mary so that our lives may give the greatest possible glory to Almighty God. No virtue is acquired in a moment or simply because one wishes to be virtuous. Virtues are acquired over time and with discipline and persistence. The external actions and prayers by which we begin to live our consecration are, for St. Louis de Montfort, like so many drops of rain upon the soil of our hearts, a rain that makes it possible for the seeds of devotion implanted within us during the process of preparation to grow and bear fruit within us. As St. Louis de Montfort uses two different arrangements in explaining the nature of these virtues – one found in *True Devotion* and the other in *Secret of Mary* – we will follow here the outline that he provides in *True Devotion*.

To do all things *through Mary* is to renounce our self-will. Our motivations are both mixed and exceedingly limited. Even our best efforts in the service of the Gospel are colored by our pride, our selfishness, our desire to be noticed, our resentments and our self-interest. The motivations of Our Lady are completely in harmony with the will of God. Our vision is limited and we can only act toward the limited good that we see in a limited way. Our Lady sees clearly and completely and well beyond the narrow limits of our sense of what is right and so she best knows how to apply and direct our actions. This is why it is important to learn to pause before acting and to renounce our intentions that we might allow ourselves to act according to those of Our Lady.

To do all things *with Mary* is to take her for our example. We do not only naturally seek to do things according to our own will but also to act in all things according to our own manner. However, we are products of a world that does not know well how to serve or to love rightly and effectively. We attempt to love, but often love wrongly. Our attempts at generosity often fall short of the mark. Our hospitality lacks a certain amount of warmth. Our Lady's welcome is never cold, nor does her generosity fail, and her love is always truly and rightly expressed. Having before our eyes the star of her example – essentially inviting her to love with us, to be generous with us, to be hospitable with us – we can begin to learn how to act in a manner that is truly pleasing to Almighty God.

To do all things *in Mary* is to have been given a special grace of the Holy Spirit. Of the great virtues of the life of consecration, this is the one that we cannot acquire through our own efforts as Mary is the "enclosed garden and sealed fountain" of God himself and one is only allowed entry into the depth of her life by a special grace of the Holy Spirit. This remarkable grace, which the Lord gives in his time to those who faithfully live the consecration, is the grace that allows us to be truly molded and formed into the likeness of the Lord Jesus Christ. Through this grace, our relationship with Our Lady is one in which she is no longer simply alongside us or with us, but one in which her life enfolds and contains our own. It is within her heart that we act generously and learn the generosity of Jesus himself. Her great faith and ardent prayerfulness become the chapel within which we kneel in worship and pray, like Christ himself, as true children of God. It is within her, where Satan has never gained entry, where we can be freed of our most persistent sins.

To do all things *for Mary* is to make it a point to bring her honor in all that we do. It is not enough for St. Louis de Montfort that we implicitly honor Our Lady. The consecrated must take the initiative in actively bringing her honor. However, this must be first and foremost a matter of our conscious internal dispositions. The more we honor Our Lady the more we act in accordance with the Spirit of Almighty God who is the first to have honored her. In honoring Our Lady we are, in fact, celebrating the great things that the Almighty has done in her and are, therefore, giving genuine glory to God. Most wondrous, however, is that when Our Lady receives any honor from us, however small it may be, she herself turns in praise and thanksgiving to glorify the Almighty One who has done great things for her. Her song of praise amplifies our small act and in the end the Lord receives much more glory than had we tried to praise him on our own. Offering simple and genuine honors to Our

Lady is the best way to cultivate this virtue – an inconvenience borne in her name or the adorning of one of her altars with flowers are fine beginnings.

One can also use these habits of the heart as reliable guides in the examination of conscience with regard to the quality of one's living of the consecration. For example: What have I done for Our Lady today? Have I tried to learn from her today? Whose spirit has been directing my decisions for the last month?

A Final Word

A GOOD BEGINNING HAS BEEN MADE. MOVE FORWARD SIMPLY AND with confidence, for victory belongs not to the swift but to the faithful. The Holy Spirit will lead us to more concrete actions if we are faithful to a simple beginning.

NOS CUM PROLE PIA BENEDICAT VIRGO MARIA
(May the Virgin Mary bless us with her loving child.)

APPENDIX

―――――

The Little Crown of the Blessed Virgin Mary

Fr. de Monfort's Prayer to Blessed Virgin

The Holy Rosary According to a Method Composed by St. Louis de Montfort

THE LITTLE CROWN
of the
BLESSED VIRGIN MARY

Leader   Allow me to praise you, O holy Virgin.
All   Give me strength against your enemies.

I. THE CROWN OF EXCELLENCE

To honor the divine maternity of the Blessed Virgin, her perpetual virginity, her sinless purity and her numberless virtues.

> Our Father
> Hail Mary

L. Blessed are you, O Virgin Mary, who bore the Lord, the Creator of the world,
A. You became the Mother of your Maker, and you remain forever virgin.

L. Rejoice, O Virgin Mary!
A. Rejoice a thousand times!

> Hail Mary

L. Holy and immaculate Virgin, I do not know fitting praises to extol you,

A. The One whom heaven cannot contain, you cloistered within your womb.

L. Rejoice, O Virgin Mary!

A. Rejoice a thousand times!

Hail Mary

L. You are all beautiful, O Virgin Mary,

A. And there is no stain within you.

L. Rejoice, O Virgin Mary!

A. Rejoice a thousand times!

Hail Mary

L. Your virtues, O Virgin, are so many

A. They outnumber the stars of heaven.

L. Rejoice, O Virgin Mary!

A. Rejoice a thousand times!

Glory be to the Father.....

II. The Crown of Power

To honor the royal authority of the Blessed Virgin, her stewardship of God's grace, her mediation and her protection of the Church.

Our Father
Hail Mary

L. Glory to you, O Queen of the whole world!
A. Bring us with you to the joys of Heaven.

L. Rejoice, O Virgin Mary!
A. Rejoice a thousand times!

Hail Mary

L. Glory to you, O Treasure House of the graces of the Lord!
A. Grant us a share in your riches.

L. Rejoice, O Virgin Mary!
A. Rejoice a thousand times!

Hail Mary

L. Glory to you, O Mediatrix between God and man!
A. Through you may the Almighty be favorable to us.

L. Rejoice, O Virgin Mary!
A. Rejoice a thousand times!

Hail Mary

L. Glory to you, O Vanquisher of heresies and demons!
A. Be for us a loving guide.

L. Rejoice, O Virgin Mary!
A. Rejoice a thousand times!

Glory be to the Father.....

III. THE CROWN OF GOODNESS

To honor the compassion of the Blessed Virgin toward sinners, the lost, the just and the dying.

Our Father
Hail Mary

L. Glory to you, O Refuge of sinners!
A. Intercede for us before the Lord.

L. Rejoice, O Virgin Mary!
A. Rejoice a thousand times!

Hail Mary

L. Glory to you, O Mother of orphans!
A. Make us pleasing to the Almighty Father.

L. Rejoice, O Virgin Mary!
A. Rejoice a thousand times!

Hail Mary

L. Glory to you, O Happiness of the just!
A. Bring us with you to the joys of Heaven.

L. Rejoice, O Virgin Mary!
A. Rejoice a thousand times!
Hail Mary

L. Glory to you, O Advocate ever present in life and in death!
A. Bring us with you to the kingdom of Heaven.

L. Rejoice, O Virgin Mary!
A. Rejoice a thousand times!

Glory be to the Father.....

CONCLUDING PRAYER

Hail Mary, beloved Daughter of God the Father.
Hail Mary, admirable Mother of God the Son.
Hail Mary, most faithful Spouse of God the Holy Spirit.
Hail Mary, august Temple of the most holy Trinity.
Hail Mary, my dear Mistress, my good Mother,
the Queen of my heart,
my life, my sweetness and my greatest hope after Jesus,
O my heart and my soul,
I am all yours, and all that I have belongs to you.

O Virgin blessed above all creation!
I beseech you that today your soul be within me
to glorify the Lord;
that your spirit be within me to rejoice in God.

O faithful Virgin!
Set yourself as a loving seal over my heart
so that through you and in you
I may be found faithful to my God.
O benign Mother!
Grant me the grace to place myself today
among those whom you love, teach, nourish, guide
and protect as your children.

O Queen of Heaven!
Do not permit there to be anything in me
that does not belong to you,
for I renounce such things from this moment.

O Daughter of the King of kings, whose principal glory is within,
do not allow me to lose myself in visible and fleeting things,
but grant that, through an abundance of grace,
I may be always attentive within myself
so that I may find in God my delight, my treasure, my honor,
my glory and my rest,
so that by the Holy Spirit, your faithful Spouse,
and you, his faithful Spouse,
Jesus Christ, your dear Son, may be perfectly formed in our hearts
to the greater glory of God our Father,
forever and ever.
Amen.

FR. DE MONTFORT'S PRAYER
to the
BLESSED VIRGIN MARY

Hail Mary, most beloved Daughter of the Eternal Father;
Hail Mary, admirable Mother of the Son;
Hail Mary, most faithful Spouse of the Holy Spirit;
Hail Mary, my dear Mother;
my amiable Mistress and my powerful Queen,
Hail, my joy, my glory, my heart and my soul!
You are all mine through mercy,
and I am all yours through justice.
But I am not yet sufficiently yours:
I give myself entirely to you once again, as an eternal slave,
with nothing reserved for myself or for any other.

If you still see in me something that does not belong to you,
I ask you to take it this moment,
and to make yourself the absolute Mistress of my powers;
to destroy, uproot and bring to nothing in me
everything that displeases God,
and there to plant, there to raise up and
there to work everything that pleases you.

May the light of your faith dispel the darkness of my mind;

may your profound humility take the place of my pride;
may your sublime contemplation stop
the distractions of my wandering imagination;
may your continual vision of God
fill my memory with his presence;
may the fire of the charity of your heart
stretch and inflame the apathy and chill of my own;
may your virtues take the place of my sins;
may your merits be my adornment
and my completion before God.
Finally, my most dear and beloved Mother, grant,
if it be possible, that I may have no other mind than yours
to know Jesus Christ and his divine will;
that I may have no other soul than yours
to praise and glorify the Lord;
that I may have no other heart than yours to love God
with a pure love and an ardent love like you.

I do not ask you for visions, or revelations,
or experiences or pleasures, even those that are spiritual.
It is yours to see clearly without darkness;
it is yours to savor fully without bitterness;
it is yours to triumph gloriously at the right-hand
of your Son in heaven without any humiliation;
it is yours to command absolutely
angels, and men and demons without resistance,
and lastly, to apply, according to your will,
all of the good things of God, without reservation.

Behold, O divine Mary,
the excellent portion that the Lord has given you,
and which will never be taken from you;

and which gives me a great joy.
For my portion, here below,
I want no other than that which you had known:
to believe purely without tasting or seeing;
to suffer joyously, without consolation from creatures;
to die continually to myself, without respite;
to work bravely, even unto death, for you,
without any interest of my own,
as the most worthless of your slaves.

The only grace I ask of you, through pure mercy,
is that every day and every moment of my life,
I may say three times, "Amen":

Amen: So be it, to all that you have done
on the earth when you lived there;
Amen: So be it, to all that you are doing now in heaven;
Amen: So be it, to all that you are doing in my soul,
so that there will be none but you to fully glorify Jesus in me,
through time and through eternity.
Amen

THE HOLY ROSARY

*According to a Method Composed by
St. Louis de Montfort*

FR. DE MONTFORT, THE GREAT APOSTLE OF THE ROSARY, composed a number of distinct methods of saying the Rosary. The particular method included here is an abridgement of a form of praying the Rosary that he had composed for use by the Daughters of Wisdom, the community of religious sisters that he founded. Variations of this method have been in continuous use among the people of God since its composition nearly three hundred years ago.

Personal Offering of the Rosary

Whether the Rosary is said privately by a single person or together by a group, begin by making a personal offering of the Rosary to the Lord Jesus Christ:

I UNITE WITH ALL THE SAINTS IN HEAVEN, WITH ALL THE JUST that are on the earth and with all the faithful souls that are present here: I unite with you, my Jesus, that I may worthily praise your holy Mother, and to praise you in her and through her. I renounce all the distractions that may come to me during this Rosary that I wish to say with modesty, attention and devotion, as if it were to be that last of my life. Amen.

Introductory Prayers

WE OFFER YOU, MOST HOLY TRINITY, THIS CREED IN ORDER TO honor all the Mysteries of our Faith; this Our Father and the three Hail Mary's in order to honor the unity of your essence, the Trinity of your Persons. We ask of you a lively faith, a firm hope and an ardent charity. Amen.

> Apostles' Creed
> Our Father
> Hail Mary (3x)
> Glory be....

The Mysteries

Fr. de Montfort recommends that in the praying of the mysteries of the Rosary, a brief word be added after the name of Jesus in each Hail Mary to honor that particular mystery. He provides this brief word in the prayers for each decade. For example: ....blessed is the fruit of thy womb, Jesus incarnate; or ....blessed is the fruit of thy womb, Jesus crowned with thorns.

Fr. de Montfort also recommends that each decade of the Rosary be introduced and concluded by means of a prayer that asks for a particular grace that is associated with the mystery that is being prayed.

First Beads
THE JOYFUL MYSTERIES

The Incarnation

We offer you, Lord Jesus, this first decade in honor of your Incarnation in the womb of Mary; and we ask of you, by this Mystery and through her intercession, a profound humility. Amen.

> Our Father
> Hail Mary (10x) adding Jesus incarnate
> Glory be.....

May the graces of the Mystery of the Incarnation come down into our souls. Amen.

The Visitation

We offer you, Lord Jesus, this second decade in honor of the Visitation of your most holy Mother to her cousin Saint Elizabeth and of the sanctification of St. John the Baptist; and we ask of you, by this Mystery and through the intercession of your holy Mother, charity toward our neighbor. Amen.

> Our Father
> Hail Mary (10x) adding Jesus sanctifying
> Glory be.....

May the graces of the Mystery of the Visitation come down into our souls. Amen.

The Birth of Jesus

We offer you, Lord Jesus, this third decade in honor of your Nativity in the Stable of Bethlehem; and we ask of you, by this Mystery and through the intercession of your holy Mother, contempt of riches and a love of poverty. Amen.

Our Father
Hail Mary (10x) adding Jesus being born
Glory be.....

May the graces of the Mystery of the Birth of Jesus come down into our souls. Amen.

The Presentation in the Temple

We offer you, Lord Jesus, this fourth decade in honor of your Presentation in the Temple and of the purification of Mary; and we ask of you, by this Mystery and through her intercession, a great purity of body and spirit. Amen.

Our Father
Hail Mary (10x) adding Jesus sacrificed
Glory be.....

May the graces of the Mystery of the Purification come down into our souls. Amen.

The Finding of Jesus

We offer you, Lord Jesus, this fifth decade in honor of your Finding by Mary; and we ask of you, by this Mystery and through her intercession, true wisdom. Amen.

Our Father
Hail Mary (10x) adding Jesus the Holy of Holies
Glory be.....

May the graces of the Mystery of the Finding of Jesus come down into our souls. Amen.

Second Beads
The Sorrowful Mysteries

The Agony

We offer you, Lord Jesus, this sixth decade in honor of your mortal Agony in the Garden of Olives; and we ask of you, by this Mystery and through the intercession of your holy Mother, contrition for our sins. Amen.

> Our Father
> Hail Mary (10x) adding Jesus Agonizing
> Glory be.....

May the graces of the Mystery of the Agony of Jesus come down into our souls. Amen.

The Scourging

We offer you, Lord Jesus, this seventh decade in honor of your bloody Scourging; and we ask of you, by this Mystery and through the intercession of your holy Mother, the mortification of our senses. Amen.

> Our Father
> Hail Mary (10x) adding Jesus scourged
> Glory be.....

May the graces of the Mystery of the Scourging of Jesus come down into our souls. Amen.

The Crowning with Thorns

We offer you, Lord Jesus, this eighth decade in honor of your Being Crowned with Thorns; and we ask of you, by this Mystery and through the intercession of your holy Mother, contempt of the world. Amen.

> Our Father
> Hail Mary (10x) adding Jesus crowned with thorns
> Glory be.....

May the graces of the Crowning with Thorns come down into our souls. Amen.

The Carrying of the Cross

We offer you, Lord Jesus, this ninth decade in honor of your Carrying of the Cross; and we ask of you, by this Mystery and through the intercession of your holy Mother, patience in all of our crosses. Amen.

> Our Father
> Hail Mary (10x) adding Jesus carrying his Cross
> Glory be.....

May the graces of the Mystery of the Carrying of the Cross come down into our souls. Amen.

The Crucifixion

We offer you, Lord Jesus, this tenth decade in honor of your Crucifixion and your ignominious death on Calvary; and we ask of you, by this Mystery and through the intercession of your holy Mother, the conversion of sinners, the perseverance of the just and the relief of the souls in Purgatory. Amen.

Our Father
Hail Mary (10x) adding Jesus crucified
Glory be.....

May the graces of the Mystery of the Crucifixion of Jesus come down into our souls. Amen.

Third Beads
THE GLORIOUS MYSTERIES

The Resurrection

We offer you, Lord Jesus, this eleventh decade in honor of your glorious Resurrection; and we ask of you, by this Mystery and through the intercession of your holy Mother, love of God and fervor in your service. Amen.

> Our Father
> Hail Mary (10x) adding Jesus risen
> Glory be.....

May the graces of the Mystery of the Resurrection come down into our souls. Amen.

The Ascension

We offer you, Lord Jesus, this twelfth decade in honor of your triumphant Ascension; and we ask of you, by this Mystery and through the intercession of your holy Mother, an ardent desire for Heaven our true home. Amen.

> Our Father
> Hail Mary (10x) adding Jesus rising to the heavens
> Glory be.....

May the graces of the Mystery of the Ascension come down into our souls. Amen.

Pentecost

We offer you, Lord Jesus, this thirteenth decade in honor of the Mystery of Pentecost; and we ask of you, by this Mystery and through the intercession of your holy Mother, the descent of the Holy Spirit into our souls. Amen.

> Our Father
> Hail Mary (10x) adding Jesus filling you with the Holy Spirit
> Glory be.....

May the graces of the Mystery of Pentecost come down into our souls. Amen.

The Assumption of the Holy Virgin

We offer you, Lord Jesus, this fourteenth decade in honor of the Resurrection and triumphant Assumption of your holy Mother into Heaven; and we ask of you, by this Mystery and through her intercession, a tender devotion to so good a Mother. Amen.

> Our Father
> Hail Mary (10x) adding Jesus raising you up
> Glory be.....

May the graces of the Mystery of the Assumption come down into our souls. Amen.

The Coronation of Mary

We offer you, Lord Jesus, this fifteenth decade in honor of the Coronation of your holy Mother; and we ask of you, by this Mystery and through her intercession, perseverance in grace and the Crown of glory. Amen.

> Our Father
> Hail Mary (10x) adding Jesus crowning you
> Glory be.....

May the graces of the Mystery of the Crowning of Mary come down into our souls. Amen.

Concluding Prayers

Hail Mary,
most beloved Daughter of the eternal Father,
admirable Mother of the Son,
most faithful Spouse of the Holy Spirit,
august Temple of the most holy Trinity.

Hail, sovereign Princess,
to whom all is subject in Heaven and on earth.
Hail, sure Refuge of sinners,
Our Lady of Mercy who has never rejected anyone,
all sinful that I am, I cast myself at your feet,
and I ask you to obtain for me from the good Jesus, your dear Son,
contrition and pardon for all of my sins along with divine wisdom.

I consecrate myself entirely to you along with all that I have.
I take you today for my Mother and my Mistress;
treat me then as the last of your children
and the most obedient of your servants.
Listen, my Princess, listen to the sighs of a heart
that desires to love you and to serve you faithfully.
Let it not be said that of all of those who have had recourse to you,
that I have been the first to be abandoned!

O my hope! O my life!
O my faithful and Immaculate Virgin Mary!
graciously hear me, defend me, nourish me, instruct me, save me.
Amen.

Praised, adored and loved be Jesus
in the most holy Sacrament of the altar. Amen.

Nos cum prole pia benedicat Virgo Maria.
(May the Virgin Mary bless us with her loving child)

Statue of Our Lady of Peace from Mount Saviour Monastery, Pine City NY.

Suggested Consecration Schedules

Date of Consecration *Feast Day*	First day of the Preparation process
January 1 *Mary, Mother of God*	November 29
February 2 *Presentation of the Lord*	December 31
February 11 *Our Lady of Lourdes*	January 9
March 25 *Annunciation of the Lord*	February 20
April 28 *St. Louis de Montfort*	March 26
May 13 *Our Lady of Fatima*	April 10
May 31 *Visitation*	April 28
August 15 *Assumption of Our Lady*	July 13
August 22 *Queenship of Mary*	July 20

SEPTEMBER 8 *Nativity of the Blessed Virgin*	AUGUST 6
SEPTEMBER 14 *Triumph of the Cross*	AUGUST 12
OCTOBER 7 *Our Lady of the Rosary*	SEPTEMBER 4
DECEMBER 8 *Immaculate Conception*	NOVEMBER 5
DECEMBER 12 *Our Lady of Guadalupe*	NOVEMBER 9
DECEMBER 25 *Nativity of Our Lord*	NOVEMBER 22

Prior to using this calendar to select a date upon which to make one's consecration, the reader is advised to revisit the *Choosing a Feast Day* discussion on page 7 of the Introduction.

NOTES

NOTES

NOTES

NOTES

NOTES

NOTES

NOTES

THE MISSIONARIES OF THE COMPANY OF MARY
(Montfort Missionaries)
AD JESUM PER MARIAM

The spiritual legacy contained within the life and writings of St. Louis de Montfort is one of the truly great treasures of the Roman Catholic Church. The task of bringing the full wealth of that treasure to the faithful is the heart of the mission of the MISSIONARIES OF THE COMPANY OF MARY (Montfort Missionaries), the community of those priests and brothers who have been consecrated to follow in his footsteps. Since our foundation by St. Louis de Montfort, the missionary activity of the Company of Mary has grown to include active apostolates serving the needs of the people of God in nearly thirty countries.

MONTFORT PUBLICATIONS is a ministry of the Company of Mary through which we make available the writings of St. Louis de Montfort and resources to assist the faithful in understanding and living the full depth of his profound spirituality.

Montfort Publications
26 South Saxon Avenue
Bay Shore, NY 11706

Phone: 631.665.0726
Email: customerservice@montfortpublications.com
Web: montfortpublications.com